ON A WONDERFUL LITTLE PLANET...

HOWTOONS

TOOLS OF MASS CONSTRUCTION!

TABLE OF CONTENTS

INTRODUCTION

Before the industrial revolution, little humans learned to be big humans by playing with the world around them. We had processes called apprenticeship and mentoring where skills and knowledge were handed down one-on-one or in small groups using physical examples and learning by practice. Then, for reasons sociological and economic, we invented the modern form of school. Lots of kids started sitting at desks, in groups, trying to learn about a three-dimensional world using two-dimensional books and blackboards. It wasn't all bad, but it certainly wasn't all good.

Howtoons got its start at Massachusetts Institute of Technology (MIT), a bastion of anarchy in education, where irreverence is valued over tradition. Here we started to believe that there had to be a better way for people to develop the basic skills of making their own toys and games, learning science and engineering along the way. Originally we were just Saul Griffith, a PhD student in engineering, and Joost Bonsen, a student at the intersection of business and technology. Quickly we realized that just technology wouldn't be enough: we need engaging art, design, and story. That is when the project was lucky enough to find Nick Dragotta, famed comic book artist, and Ingrid Dragotta, industrial designer and toy industry specialist. Joost ended up finding other projects to focus on, and Arwen Griffith joined the group as editor and wordsmith. Finally we had that special team with a magical combination of skills so we could all focus on our shared passion: presenting science, art, engineering and all of the related disciplines as the adventures (and misadventures) that they are and can be. We began to invite children into our world of creative exploration, fun, tools, and explosions to learn that the world need not be only what they see, but that it could be whatever they want to make it.

10 years in and we are still doing it, loving the creative challenge. We are now united by what we see as the possibility of all of this making of stuff. The potential of a curriculum of toys, a set of experiences and projects that teach all of the basic skills: tool use, different materials, and an intuition for basic physics, math, design, art, and engineering. This curriculum of toys can assist to bring modern education back from the brink, to put hands-on projects back in the hands of students so they can directly manipulate and connect to the wonderful three-dimensional world around us.

This way of looking at the world has been liberating; the world is the classroom. A playground is the first place you learn physics. A swing set is a pendulum to be studied while enjoyed. A see-saw represents a lever at its most basic, a ride-on lesson. A slide is a whooping experiment in friction and gravity. The world we all want to live in will not build itself. It needs us to invent it, to create it. We need every generation to be enabled to create their world. It starts with creativity and inventing one's own toys and games. It involves knowledge of tools, materials, and process. It will be beautiful as we marry the art with the science, and the design with the engineering. Come play with us.

"PLAY IS THE HIGHEST FORM OF RESEARCH."
- ALBERT EINSTEIN

PLAY

Some scientists wonder why we play. Not just we humans, but the royal we … mammals. Why do bear cubs and lions play? Why do chimpanzees and capuchin monkeys play? While they do not know the exact reasons yet, scientists are pretty sure that play is one of the best ways to learn. We learn through repetition, and it is much easier to repetitively do things that are fun, than try to do over and over again things that are boring. When humans reach adulthood, they often feel guilty about play, they feel like they should be working. That is our greatest mistake, forgetting to play! The most important thing to learn as a child is to continue through-out your life to be child-like, to enjoy play, to play for play's sake. Throw balls and watch how they land. Skip stones on the smooth surface of a lake. Wonder why trees grow the way they do as you climb them and why the leaves are different colors. Imagine civi-lizations beyond our galaxy. Walk on stilts to learn about the center of mass and pendu-lums. Spin tops to understand rotary motion. Play with pup-pets to understand robotic controls. Balance on a board to understand levers. The keys to understanding the world are beneath your feet and at your fingertips. They look like toys and games and playful activities.

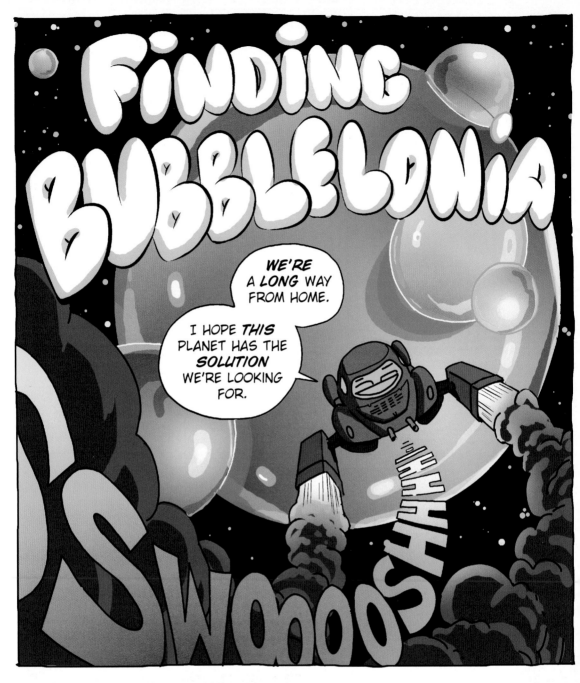

BACK AT THE LAB, THE SCIENTIFIC METHOD BEGINS.

CELINE COLLECTS DATA THROUGH OBSERVATION AND EXPERIMENTATION, FORMULATING AND TESTING HER HYPOTHESIS.

UNTIL...

BUBBLES!

YOU *DID* IT *CELINE!*

THE *KEY* WAS TO REALIZE THAT THE SOAP FORMS A *SKIN* LAYER ON EITHER SIDE OF THE WATER.

"BUBBLES EXIST WHEN THE *AIR PRESSURE* INSIDE THE BUBBLE IS IN PERFECT *BALANCE* WITH THE AIR PRESSURE *OUTSIDE* OF THE BUBBLE."

"THE SOAP, CALLED A *LIPID*, MAKES A THIN LAYER PROTECTING THE WATER."

ONE LAYER ON EACH SIDE IS WHY SCIENTISTS CALL THIS A LIPID BILAYER."

LIPID
WATER
LIPID

"I BROKE DOWN THE *INGREDIENTS* FOR..."

(THE ULTIMATE) BUBBLE SOLUTION

— 10 CUPS OF WATER

— 1 CUP OF DISH SOAP

— 1/4 CUP OF GLYCERIN (PURCHASE AT DRUG STORE)

17

Summer Games

"GAMES LUBRICATE THE BODY AND THE MIND" —BEN FRANKLIN

BALLOONS

PLASTIC BOTTLES

CHUCK IT

SQUIRT

HOLLOW PEN

SQUEEZE TO FIRE

PINCH TO STOP

SNIP

PULL BALLOON OVER CAP

TIE-WRAP BALLOON

HIGH PRESSURE

SOAK

NO JOKE

DRAGO

ENDLESS POSSIBILITIES, **HOWTOONS!**

TOPS HIT

CUT OUT AND TAPE ON TOP OF CD

CUT OUT AND TAPE ON TOP OF CD

22

Legend of the
Monkey Fist Clan

*Always employ an experienced adult in the choice of a tree and installation of a tree swing.

A shipwrecked family of seafaring arborists, the Monkey Fist Clan had to survive on a deserted island with nothing but their knot-tying tricks and rope skills to aid them.

In order to survive they learned to use rope for everything; their braids, knots, splices and weaves transformed the desolate environment into a treehouse paradise.

To throw their ropes, the clan developed a heaving knot, the Monkey's Fist. Mastery of this decorative, yet functional, knot was the first sign of adulthood.

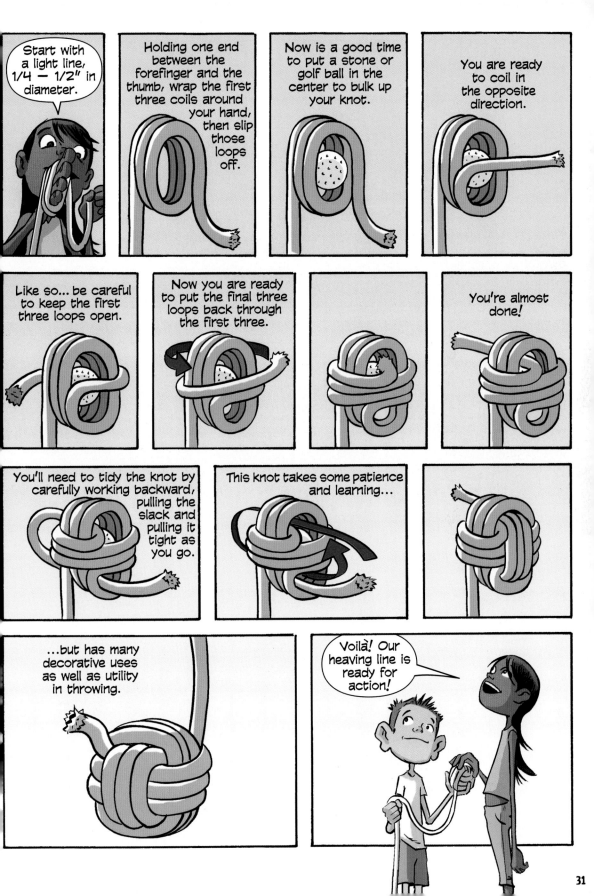

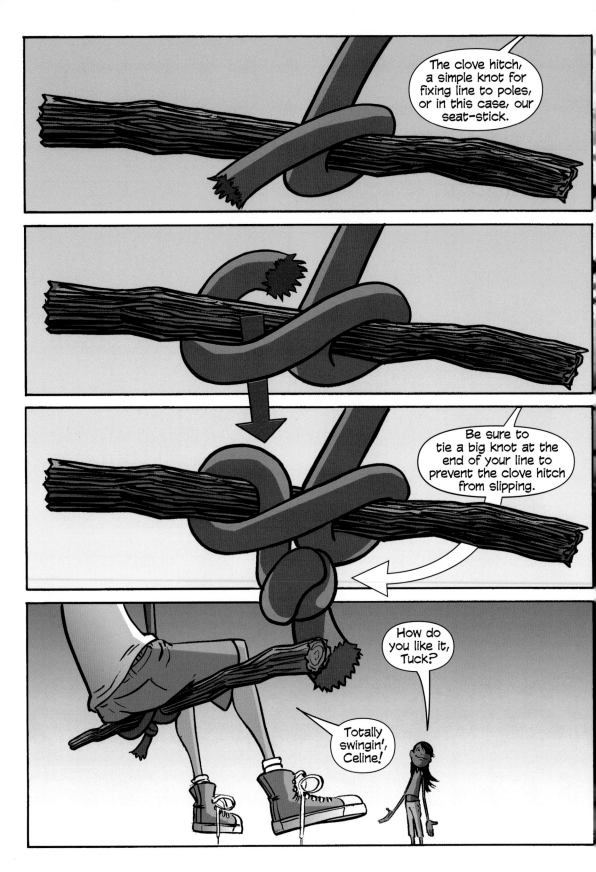

38

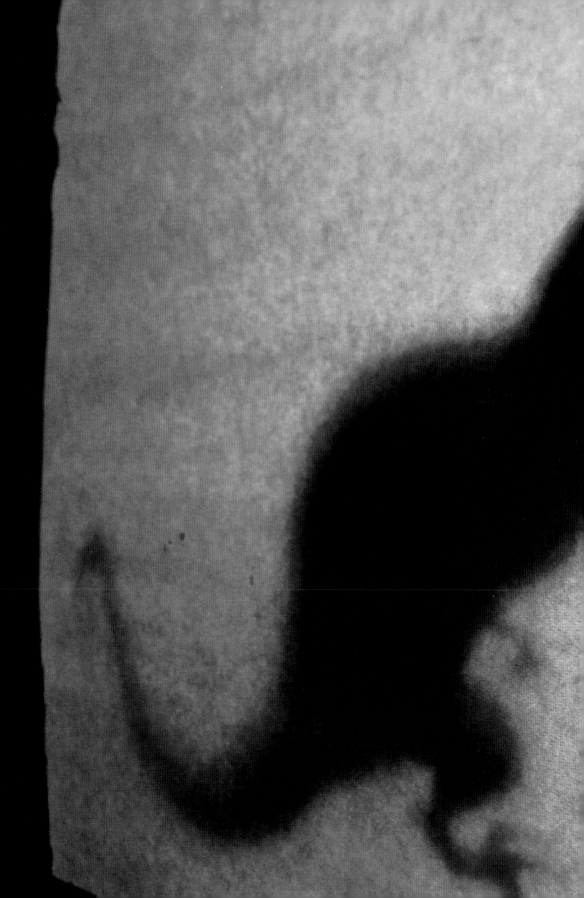

WRITTEN BY WARREN SIMONS

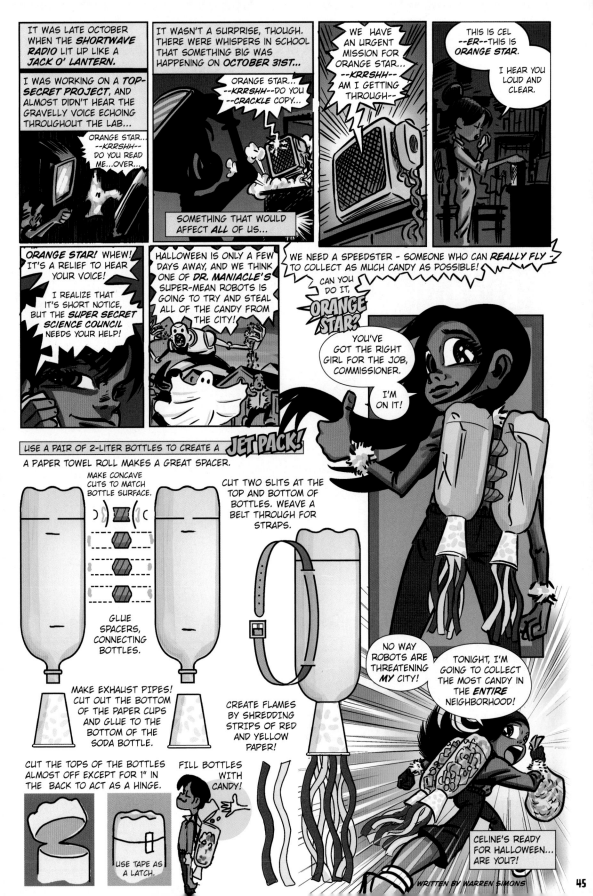

IT WAS LATE OCTOBER WHEN THE **SHORTWAVE RADIO** LIT UP LIKE A **JACK O' LANTERN.**

I WAS WORKING ON A **TOP-SECRET PROJECT,** AND ALMOST DIDN'T HEAR THE GRAVELLY VOICE ECHOING THROUGHOUT THE LAB...

ORANGE STAR... --KRRSHH-- DO YOU READ ME...OVER...

IT WASN'T A SURPRISE, THOUGH. THERE WERE WHISPERS IN SCHOOL THAT SOMETHING BIG WAS HAPPENING ON **OCTOBER 31ST**...

ORANGE STAR... --KRRSHH--DO YOU --CRACKLE COPY...

SOMETHING THAT WOULD AFFECT **ALL** OF US...

WE HAVE AN URGENT MISSION FOR ORANGE STAR... --KRRSHH-- AM I GETTING THROUGH--

THIS IS CEL --ER--THIS IS **ORANGE STAR.**

I HEAR YOU LOUD AND CLEAR.

ORANGE STAR! WHEW! IT'S A RELIEF TO HEAR YOUR VOICE!

I REALIZE THAT IT'S SHORT NOTICE, BUT THE **SUPER SECRET SCIENCE COUNCIL** NEEDS YOUR HELP!

HALLOWEEN IS ONLY A FEW DAYS AWAY, AND WE THINK ONE OF **DR. MANIACLE'S** SUPER-MEAN ROBOTS IS GOING TO TRY AND STEAL ALL OF THE CANDY FROM THE CITY!

WE NEED A SPEEDSTER - SOMEONE WHO CAN **REALLY FLY** - TO COLLECT AS MUCH CANDY AS POSSIBLE!

CAN YOU DO IT, **ORANGE STAR?**

YOU'VE GOT THE RIGHT GIRL FOR THE JOB, COMMISSIONER.

I'M ON IT!

USE A PAIR OF 2-LITER BOTTLES TO CREATE A **JET PACK!**

A PAPER TOWEL ROLL MAKES A GREAT SPACER.

MAKE CONCAVE CUTS TO MATCH BOTTLE SURFACE.

GLUE SPACERS, CONNECTING BOTTLES.

CUT TWO SLITS AT THE TOP AND BOTTOM OF BOTTLES. WEAVE A BELT THROUGH FOR STRAPS.

MAKE EXHAUST PIPES! CUT OUT THE BOTTOM OF THE PAPER CUPS AND GLUE TO THE BOTTOM OF THE SODA BOTTLE.

CREATE FLAMES BY SHREDDING STRIPS OF RED AND YELLOW PAPER!

NO WAY ROBOTS ARE THREATENING **MY** CITY!

TONIGHT, I'M GOING TO COLLECT THE MOST CANDY IN THE **ENTIRE** NEIGHBORHOOD!

CUT THE TOPS OF THE BOTTLES ALMOST OFF EXCEPT FOR 1" IN THE BACK TO ACT AS A HINGE.

FILL BOTTLES WITH CANDY!

USE TAPE AS A LATCH.

CELINE'S READY FOR HALLOWEEN... ARE YOU?!

WRITTEN BY WARREN SIMONS

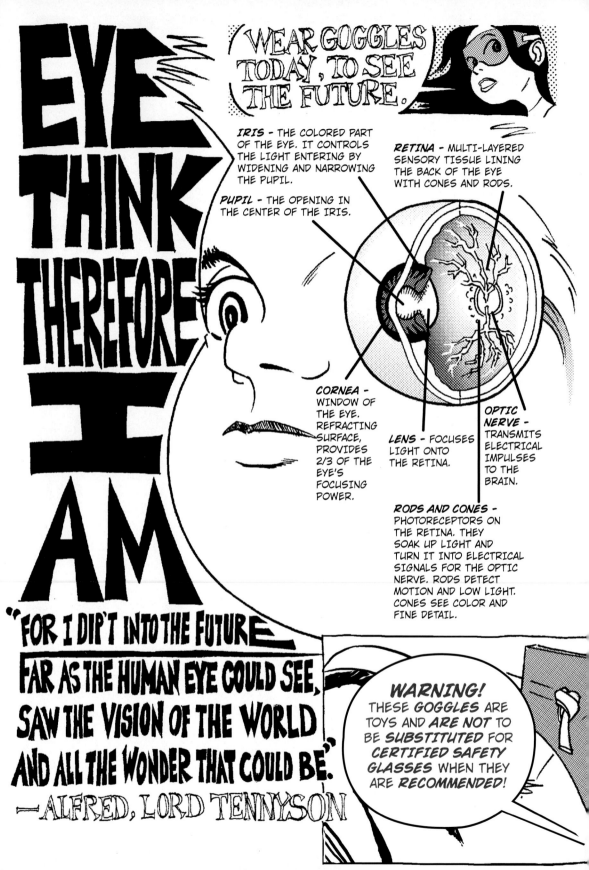

EYE THINK THEREFORE I AM

WEAR GOGGLES TODAY, TO SEE THE FUTURE.

IRIS – THE COLORED PART OF THE EYE. IT CONTROLS THE LIGHT ENTERING BY WIDENING AND NARROWING THE PUPIL.

PUPIL – THE OPENING IN THE CENTER OF THE IRIS.

RETINA – MULTI-LAYERED SENSORY TISSUE LINING THE BACK OF THE EYE WITH CONES AND RODS.

CORNEA – WINDOW OF THE EYE. REFRACTING SURFACE, PROVIDES 2/3 OF THE EYE'S FOCUSING POWER.

LENS – FOCUSES LIGHT ONTO THE RETINA.

OPTIC NERVE – TRANSMITS ELECTRICAL IMPULSES TO THE BRAIN.

RODS AND CONES – PHOTORECEPTORS ON THE RETINA. THEY SOAK UP LIGHT AND TURN IT INTO ELECTRICAL SIGNALS FOR THE OPTIC NERVE. RODS DETECT MOTION AND LOW LIGHT. CONES SEE COLOR AND FINE DETAIL.

"FOR I DIP'T INTO THE FUTURE FAR AS THE HUMAN EYE COULD SEE, SAW THE VISION OF THE WORLD AND ALL THE WONDER THAT COULD BE." —ALFRED, LORD TENNYSON

WARNING! THESE **GOGGLES** ARE TOYS AND **ARE NOT** TO BE **SUBSTITUTED** FOR **CERTIFIED SAFETY GLASSES** WHEN THEY ARE **RECOMMENDED!**

47

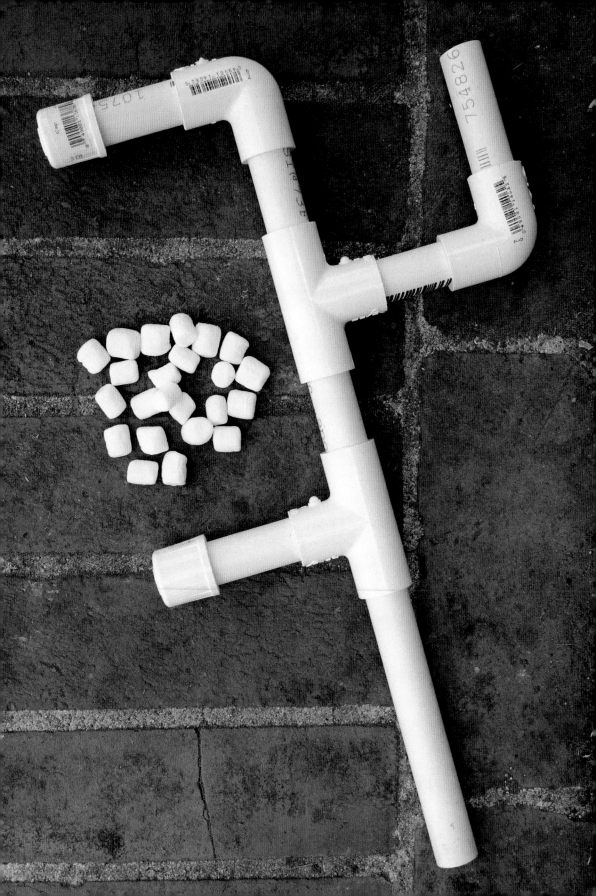

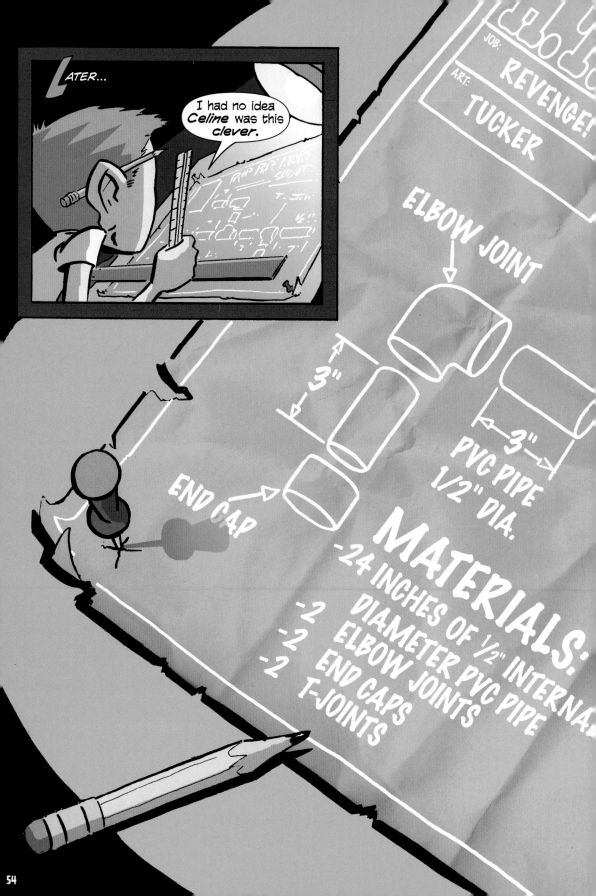

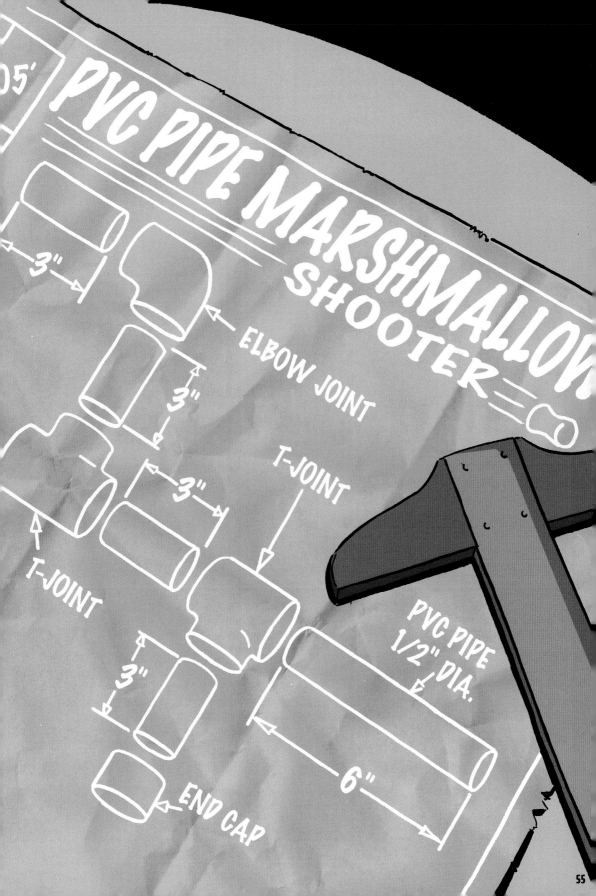

PVC PIPE MARSHMALLOW SHOOTER

5'

3"

ELBOW JOINT

3"

T-JOINT

3"

T-JOINT

PVC PIPE
1/2" DIA.

3"

6"

END CAP

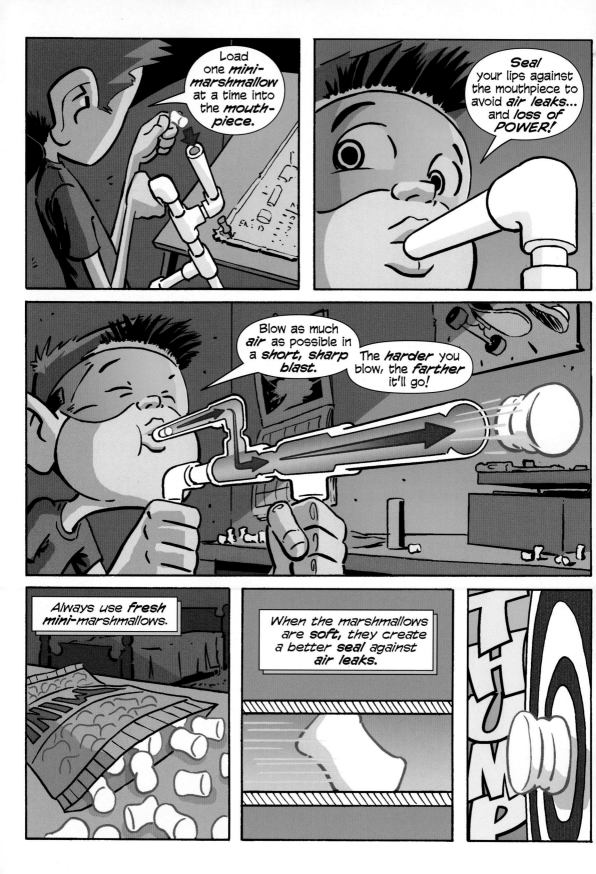

"DON'T BE A SILLY FOOL. ALWAYS USE THE RIGHT TOOL."
 – ROSS GRIFFITH (SAUL'S DAD)

TOOLS

Humans were lucky enough to win the mammalian lottery and get opposable thumbs. Lions got sharp teeth and kangaroos got awesome tails. It looks like opposable thumbs and our big brains were the major prize, though. Our brains could conceive of tools that our fabulous little hands and thumbs could manipulate to do amazing things! With these tools we built civilization as we know it. Fire, spears, wheels, rope, hammers, knives, nets and nails. To master tools and their use is to gain a lifetime of skills and be able to tackle any problem or challenge with the biggest possible toolbox. Once you have conquered the tools that already exist, the master builder can invent new tools, specific to a task or purpose, and enable new things that were not possible before.

All tools need to be treated with respect: respect for their origins, respect for the work they can do used correctly, and most importantly, respect for the damage and injuries they can inflict if used without care. Learn to use all the tools, use the right tool for the right job, always put tools back, and keep them sharp, oiled, and ready for new adventures in making.

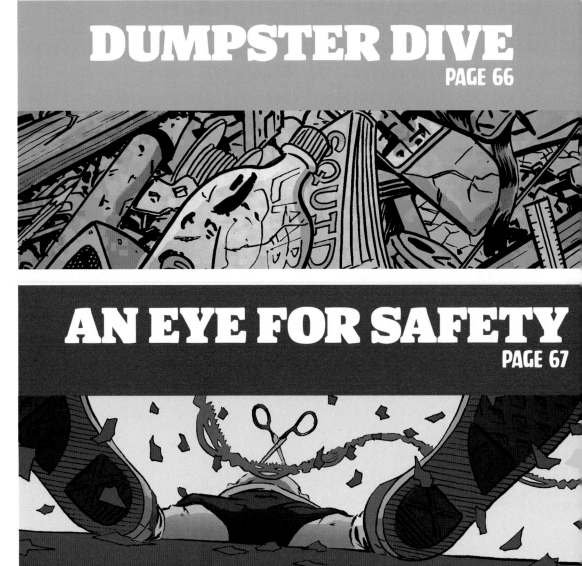

THE WORKSHOP

EVERY KID NEEDS A SPACE.

Hmmm. Where do we start?

Says here we'll need a workshop.

VIRGINIA WOOLF DESCRIBED IT AS "A ROOM OF ONE'S OWN."

HOW TO MAKE THINGS OTHER THAN TROU...

IT DOESN'T HAVE TO BE A ROOM, IT COULD BE HALF A ROOM, OR A CORNER, OR EVEN JUST A CUPBOARD, OR A SINGLE SHELF.

What do you think about *THIS* place?

THE IMPORTANT THING IS THAT IT'S A PLACE FOR YOUR BOOKS, DRAWINGS, TOOLS, TREASURES AND PROJECTS.

With a little clean up...it's perfect!

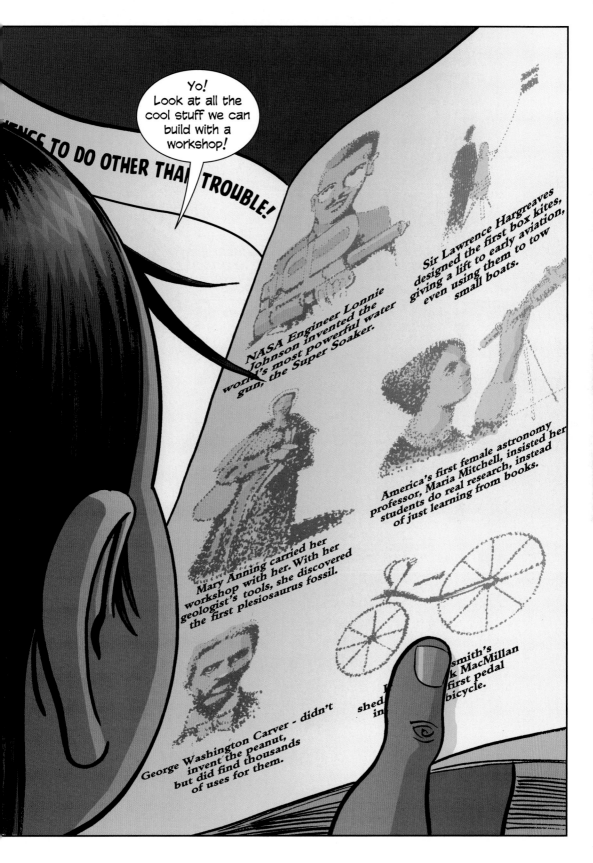

A MUSEUM OF YOUR MOST FANTASTIC FAILURES AND TREMENDOUS TRIUMPHS!

O RGANIZE YOUR SPACE! MAKE YOUR MAKING EASY, SAFE, FUN AND PRODUCTIVE. ALWAYS BE PREPARED FOR THAT NEW PROJECT.

B UT...DON'T LET IT GET TOO CLEAN — YOU'LL WANT TO FEEL FREE TO MAKE A MESS. OOH, AND HOW YOU WILL WANT TO MAKE SOME TERRIBLE MESSES.

THERE ARE MANY, MANY, MANY PROJECTS TO UNDERTAKE...

...AND IN THE CRACKS OF THOSE PROJECTS AND BENEATH THE FILTHY UNDERBELLY OF YOUR LATEST FRUSTRATION IS SOMETHING SPECIAL...

...YOUR LATEST INVENTION!

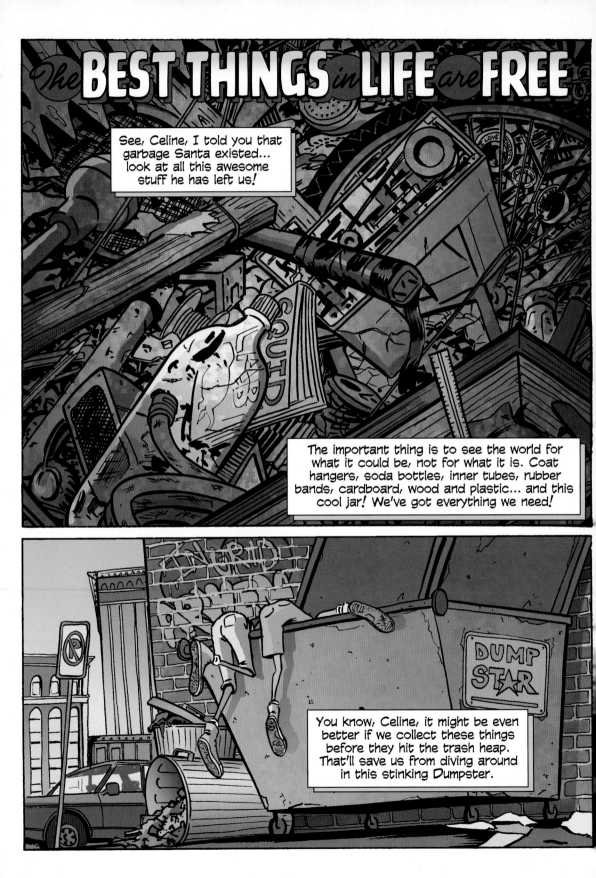

The BEST THINGS in LIFE are FREE

See, Celine, I told you that garbage Santa existed... look at all this awesome stuff he has left us!

The important thing is to see the world for what it could be, not for what it is. Coat hangers, soda bottles, inner tubes, rubber bands, cardboard, wood and plastic... and this cool jar! We've got everything we need!

DUMP STAR

You know, Celine, it might be even better if we collect these things before they hit the trash heap. That'll save us from diving around in this stinking Dumpster.

An Eye for Safety

THE BEST DEFENSE IS A GOOD IMAGINATION!

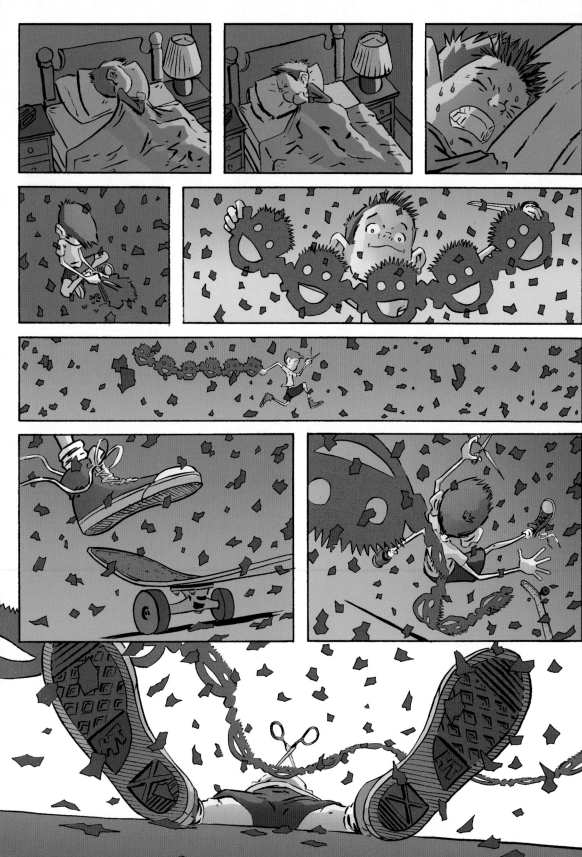

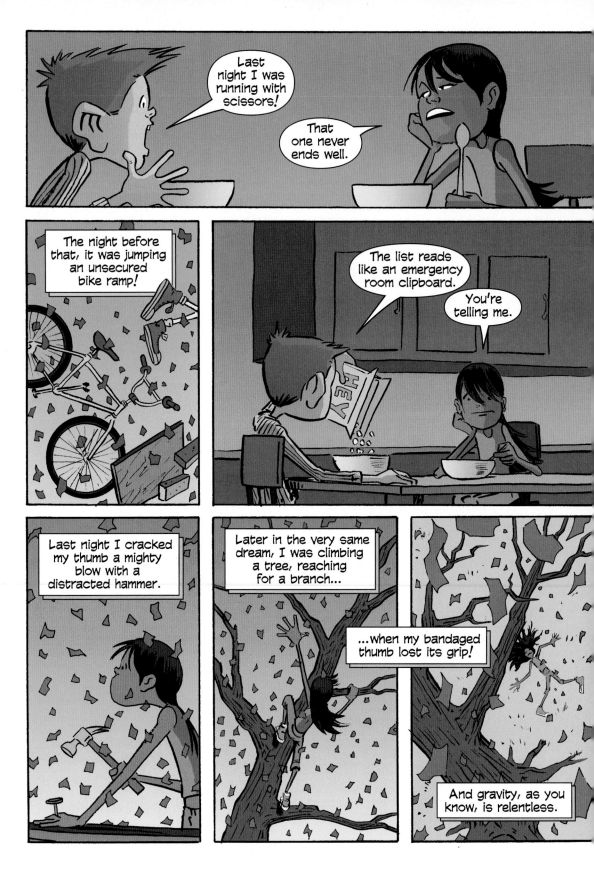

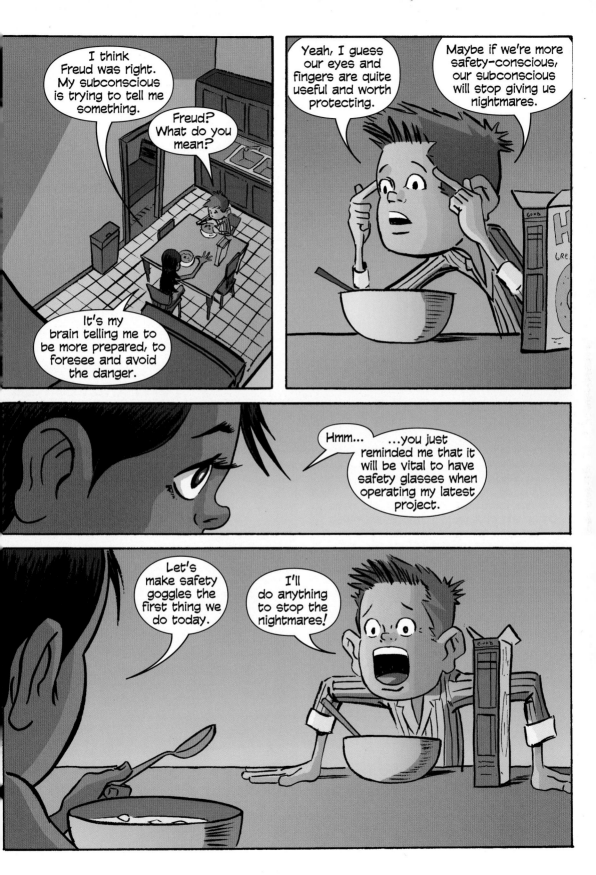

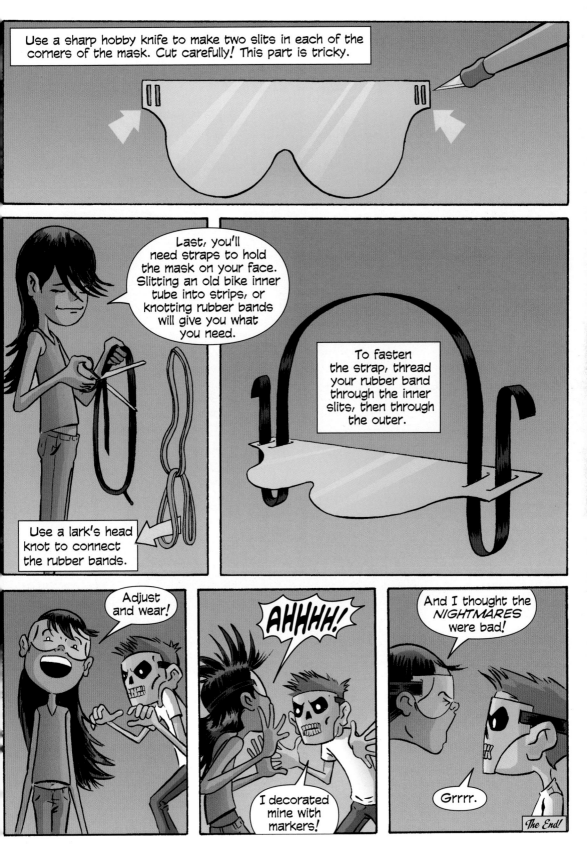

ANATOMY OF A TOOL BUCKET

A STURDY PLASTIC BUCKET IS LIKE A PORTABLE WORKSHOP. ONE WITH A STRONG WIRE HANDLE IS GOOD. YOU CAN WRAP THINGS AROUND THE HANDLE TO MAKE IT EASIER TO CARRY.

HAMMER, SCREWDRIVERS, RULER, PLIERS, CUTTERS, SCISSORS, WRENCHES, CLAMPS, FILES, PENCILS AND BRUSHES, ADD A DRILL AND YOU ARE READY TO REPAIR, CREATE AND INVENT!

YOU CAN BEND HOOKS FROM COATHANGERS TO HANG USEFUL ITEMS LIKE ROPE AND CORD FROM THE SIDE OF YOUR BUCKET.

ALWAYS KEEP A ROLL OF DUCT TAPE AND A ROLL OF WIRE HANDY.

KEEP YOUR TOOLS SHARP, OIL THE JOINTS AND BEARINGS AND WIPE THEM CLEAN. DON'T DISCARD OLD TOOLS, THEY ARE OFTEN THE BEST, AND BROKEN TOOLS CAN BE USEFUL TOO. SOMETIMES YOU CAN CONVERT A BROKEN TOOL INTO A NEW TOOL FOR AN UNUSUAL JOB. IT HELPS TO WRITE YOUR NAME OR INITIALS ON YOUR TOOLS SO YOU CAN SHARE THEM WITHOUT CONFUSION.

ORGANIZE YOUR BUCKET TO EASILY LAY YOUR HANDS ON YOUR TOOLS. LIKE AN OLD WESTERN GUN-SLINGER, YOU SHOULD BE READY TO PULL THE PERFECT TOOL FOR THE JOB AT THE RIGHT MOMENT AS A MERE REFLEX. OLD JARS OR THE BOTTOM HALF OF SODA BOTTLES CAN BE USED TO SORT THE TOOLS INSIDE THE BUCKET.

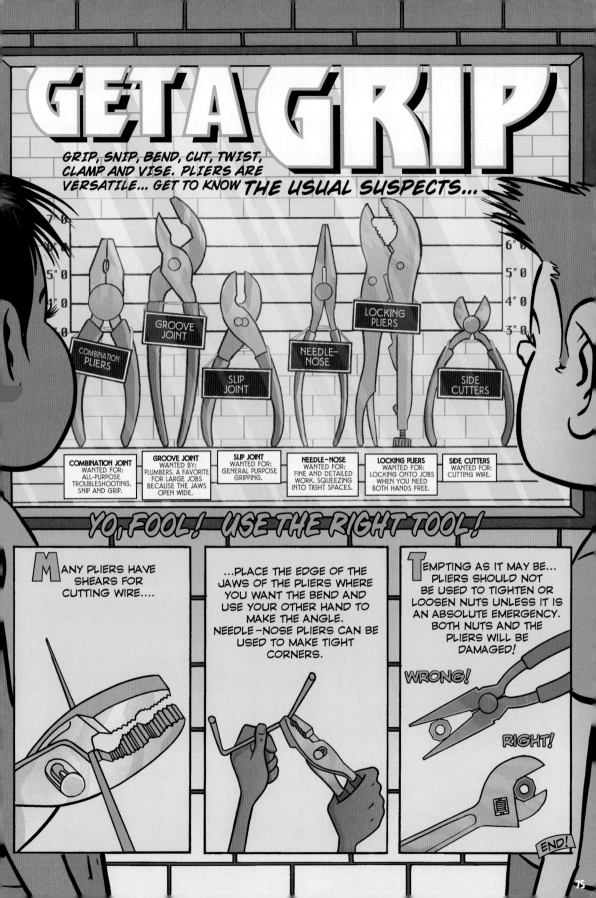

GET A GRIP

GRIP, SNIP, BEND, CUT, TWIST, CLAMP AND VISE. PLIERS ARE VERSATILE... GET TO KNOW **THE USUAL SUSPECTS...**

COMBINATION PLIERS

GROOVE JOINT

SLIP JOINT

NEEDLE-NOSE

LOCKING PLIERS

SIDE CUTTERS

COMBINATION JOINT
WANTED FOR:
ALL-PURPOSE
TROUBLESHOOTING,
SNIP AND GRIP.

GROOVE JOINT
WANTED BY:
PLUMBERS. A FAVORITE
FOR LARGE JOBS
BECAUSE THE JAWS
OPEN WIDE.

SLIP JOINT
WANTED FOR:
GENERAL PURPOSE
GRIPPING.

NEEDLE-NOSE
WANTED FOR:
FINE AND DETAILED
WORK, SQUEEZING
INTO TIGHT SPACES.

LOCKING PLIERS
WANTED FOR:
LOCKING ONTO JOBS
WHEN YOU NEED
BOTH HANDS FREE.

SIDE CUTTERS
WANTED FOR:
CUTTING WIRE.

YO, FOOL! USE THE RIGHT TOOL!

MANY PLIERS HAVE SHEARS FOR CUTTING WIRE....

...PLACE THE EDGE OF THE JAWS OF THE PLIERS WHERE YOU WANT THE BEND AND USE YOUR OTHER HAND TO MAKE THE ANGLE. NEEDLE-NOSE PLIERS CAN BE USED TO MAKE TIGHT CORNERS.

TEMPTING AS IT MAY BE... PLIERS SHOULD NOT BE USED TO TIGHTEN OR LOOSEN NUTS UNLESS IT IS AN ABSOLUTE EMERGENCY. BOTH NUTS AND THE PLIERS WILL BE DAMAGED!

WRONG!

RIGHT!

END!

CUT TO THE POINT

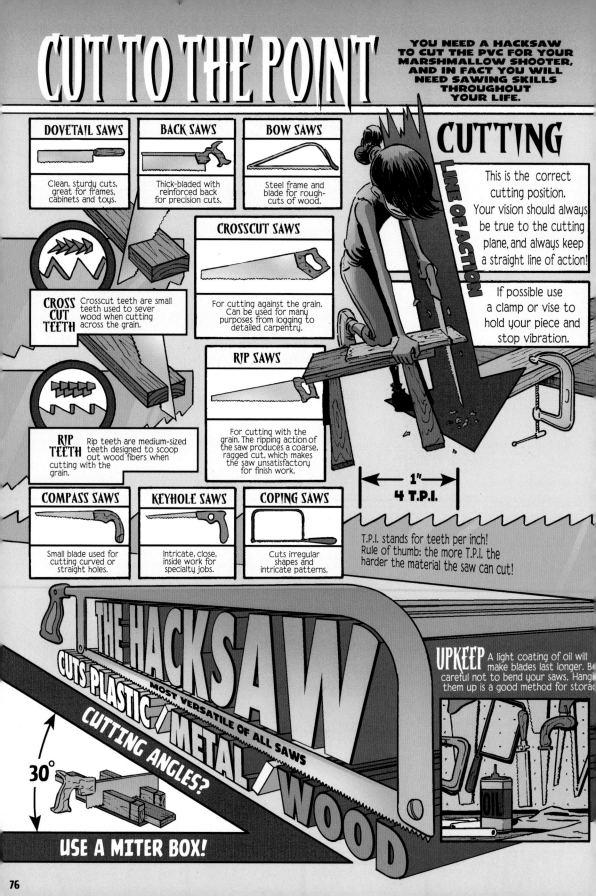

YOU NEED A HACKSAW TO CUT THE PVC FOR YOUR MARSHMALLOW SHOOTER, AND IN FACT YOU WILL NEED SAWING SKILLS THROUGHOUT YOUR LIFE.

DOVETAIL SAWS
Clean, sturdy cuts, great for frames, cabinets and toys.

BACK SAWS
Thick-bladed with reinforced back for precision cuts.

BOW SAWS
Steel frame and blade for rough-cuts of wood.

CROSSCUT SAWS
For cutting against the grain. Can be used for many purposes from logging to detailed carpentry.

CROSS CUT TEETH — Crosscut teeth are small teeth used to sever wood when cutting across the grain.

RIP SAWS
For cutting with the grain. The ripping action of the saw produces a coarse, ragged cut, which makes the saw unsatisfactory for finish work.

RIP TEETH — Rip teeth are medium-sized teeth designed to scoop out wood fibers when cutting with the grain.

COMPASS SAWS
Small blade used for cutting curved or straight holes.

KEYHOLE SAWS
Intricate, close, inside work for specialty jobs.

COPING SAWS
Cuts irregular shapes and intricate patterns.

CUTTING

LINE OF ACTION

This is the correct cutting position. Your vision should always be true to the cutting plane, and always keep a straight line of action!

If possible use a clamp or vise to hold your piece and stop vibration.

1"
4 T.P.I.

T.P.I. stands for teeth per inch! Rule of thumb: the more T.P.I. the harder the material the saw can cut!

THE HACKSAW
MOST VERSATILE OF ALL SAWS

CUTS PLASTIC / METAL / WOOD

UPKEEP A light coating of oil will make blades last longer. Be careful not to bend your saws. Hanging them up is a good method for storage.

OIL

CUTTING ANGLES?
30°

USE A MITER BOX!

"THE FUTURE IS GREEN ENERGY."
   – ARNOLD SCHWARZENEGGER
      AKA "THE TERMINATOR"

ENERGY

You wouldn't be entirely wrong in imagining energy as a seemingly magical invisible fabric that holds the whole universe together. It is why so many mythologies are littered with references to energies and forces. It's why people say important and riddle-like things about energy such as "It can neither be created, nor destroyed." Without energy, there would be nothing: no motion, no stuff, no nothing, not even you. Without energy, there would be no fun. At all. Energy is everywhere, and it's wonderfully useful. Nothing can be done without energy moving some way or the other, so to know how energy moves helps you understand pretty much all things in the universe. Energy can be embodied in many forms: in peanuts, in sunshine, in rubber bands, in the wind, in sound, in a skateboard on a hillside, in a zipline and in things that spin. There are myriad ways to harness energy (it can't technically be created), and there are myriad ways to use energy by transforming it. The really good news is that both harnessing and transforming energy can be a blast! There is no better way to build your understanding of the workings of the whole universe than by harnessing the stuff that makes it run, and repurposing it for some plain old-fashioned, high-energy fun.

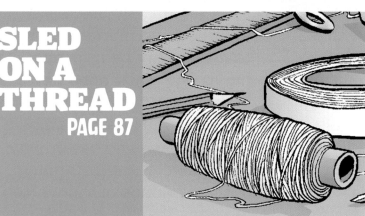

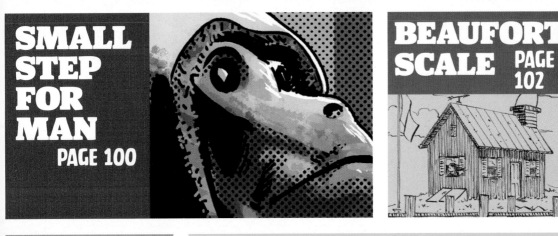

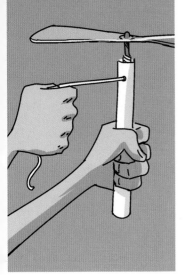

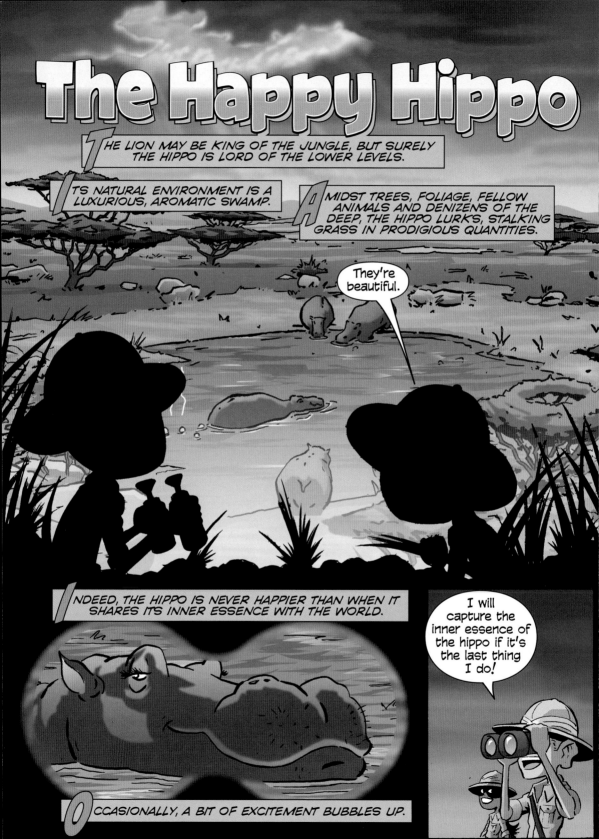

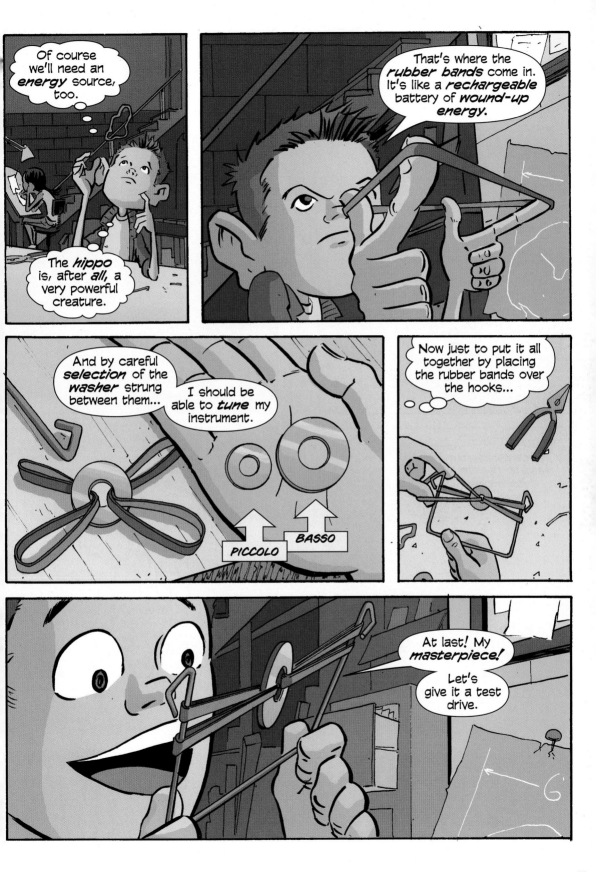

THE SIMPLEST AND EASIEST MATERIAL FOR KITE MAKING IS TYVEK. IT DOESN'T REQUIRE STITCHING, JUST TYVEK TAPE. IT CAN BE PURCHASED IN HARDWARE STORES OR FOUND AT CONSTRUCTION SITES. THE OTHER MATERIALS YOU'LL NEED ARE...

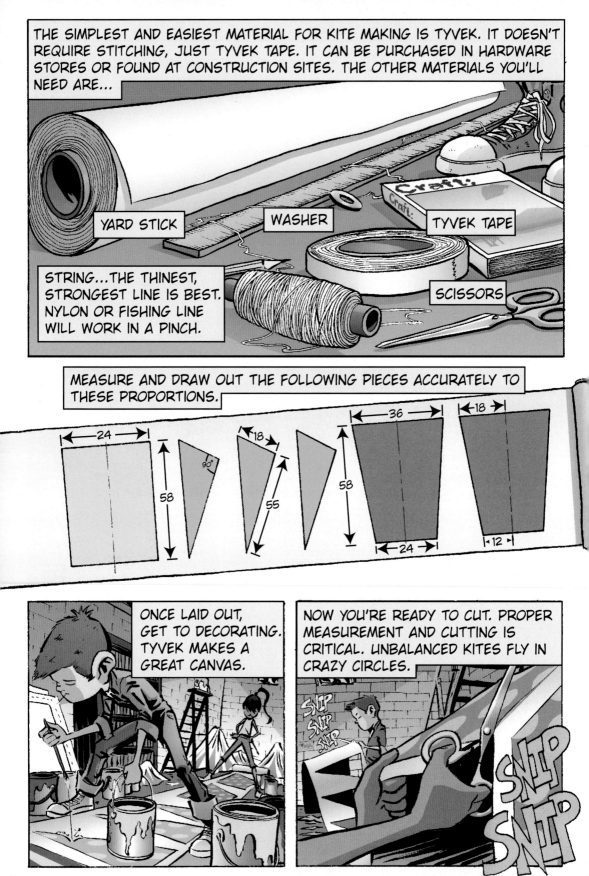

YARD STICK

WASHER

TYVEK TAPE

STRING...THE THINEST, STRONGEST LINE IS BEST. NYLON OR FISHING LINE WILL WORK IN A PINCH.

SCISSORS

MEASURE AND DRAW OUT THE FOLLOWING PIECES ACCURATELY TO THESE PROPORTIONS.

ONCE LAID OUT, GET TO DECORATING. TYVEK MAKES A GREAT CANVAS.

NOW YOU'RE READY TO CUT. PROPER MEASUREMENT AND CUTTING IS CRITICAL. UNBALANCED KITES FLY IN CRAZY CIRCLES.

SNIP SNIP SNIP

SNIP SNIP

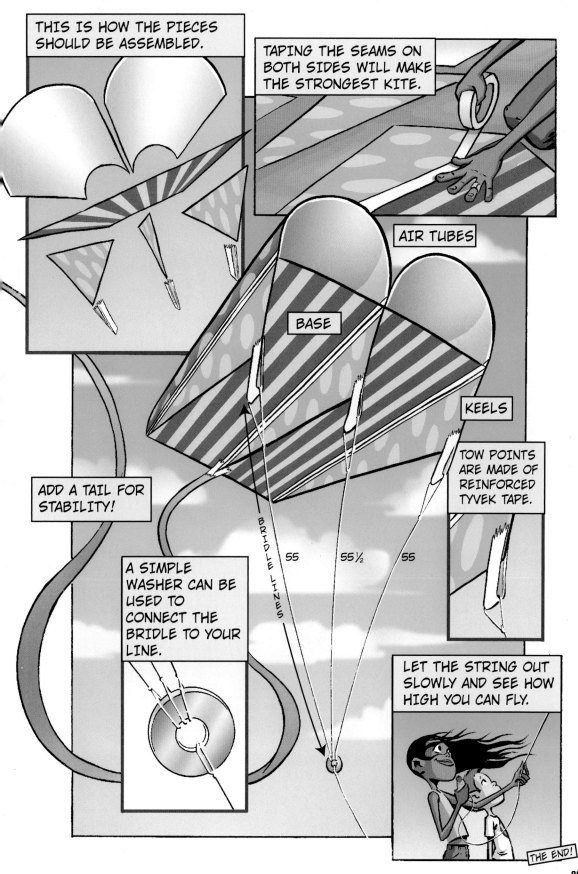

THIS IS HOW THE PIECES SHOULD BE ASSEMBLED.

TAPING THE SEAMS ON BOTH SIDES WILL MAKE THE STRONGEST KITE.

AIR TUBES

BASE

KEELS

TOW POINTS ARE MADE OF REINFORCED TYVEK TAPE.

ADD A TAIL FOR STABILITY!

BRIDLE LINES

55   55½   55

A SIMPLE WASHER CAN BE USED TO CONNECT THE BRIDLE TO YOUR LINE.

LET THE STRING OUT SLOWLY AND SEE HOW HIGH YOU CAN FLY.

THE END!

89

$$(\text{prototyping} + \text{engineering})^{\text{imagination}} = \text{better future}$$

$$\left(\frac{\text{dreaming}^2 + \text{experiment}}{\sqrt{\text{failure}} \times \text{renewal}}\right) = \text{invention}$$

SPOOL RACER

$$\text{passion} + \text{education} + \text{hard work} > \text{complacency}$$

$$\text{elegance} = f(\text{science, design})$$

$$\text{instincts} = \sum (\text{experience} + \text{knowledge})$$

$$\int \text{hard work } d \text{ opportunity} = \text{success}$$

$$\forall \text{ problems } \exists \text{ a solution } \in \text{brain}$$

DRAGOTTA 2011

① Make some snips and some slits in a square.

Cut 4 slits a ¼" from corner.

4"

2"

4"

NO LONGER WILL WE PASS GAS ONTO THE NEXT GENERATION.
THE TIME IS NOW FOR ...
ENERGY INDEPENDENCE!

THE *D.O.E. CAN'T WAIT TO CATCH A **WHIFF** OF THIS **RESEARCH**.

*The D.O.E.(Department of Energy) is responsible for developing research into sustainable alternative fuel sources – including biological sources of power.

HOWTOONS

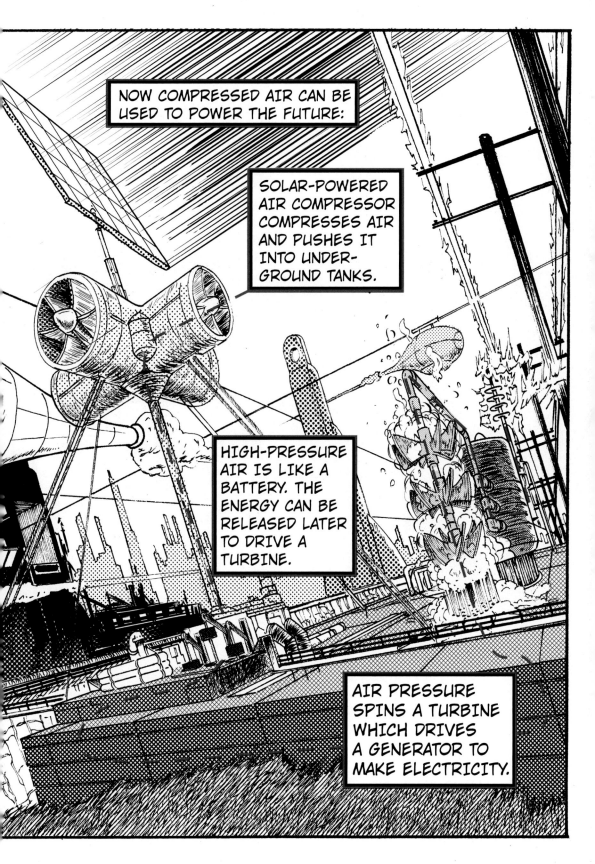

NOW COMPRESSED AIR CAN BE USED TO POWER THE FUTURE:

SOLAR-POWERED AIR COMPRESSOR COMPRESSES AIR AND PUSHES IT INTO UNDER-GROUND TANKS.

HIGH-PRESSURE AIR IS LIKE A BATTERY. THE ENERGY CAN BE RELEASED LATER TO DRIVE A TURBINE.

AIR PRESSURE SPINS A TURBINE WHICH DRIVES A GENERATOR TO MAKE ELECTRICITY.

SMALL STEP FOR MAN

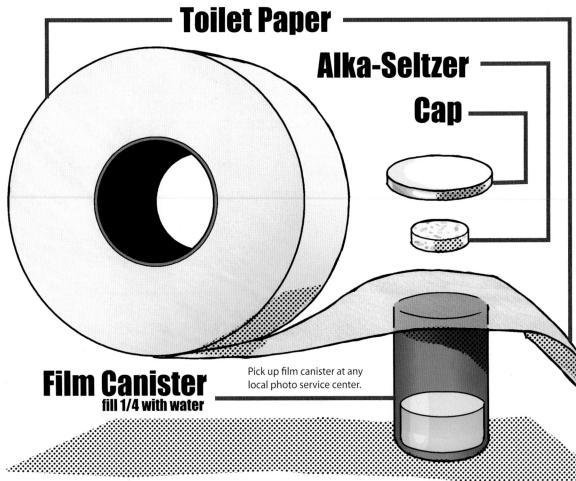

Toilet Paper

Alka-Seltzer

Cap

Film Canister
fill 1/4 with water

Pick up film canister at any local photo service center.

CLOSE THE LID

TEAR AWAY EXCESS T.P.

FLIP OVER

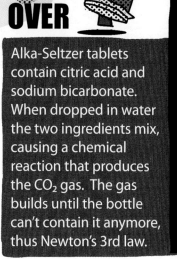

Alka-Seltzer tablets contain citric acid and sodium bicarbonate. When dropped in water the two ingredients mix, causing a chemical reaction that produces the CO_2 gas. The gas builds until the bottle can't contain it anymore, thus Newton's 3rd law.

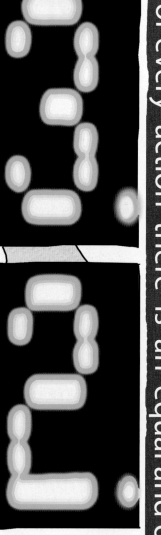

"For every action there is an equal and opposite reaction."

Sir Isaac Newton

POP

The Beaufort Scale

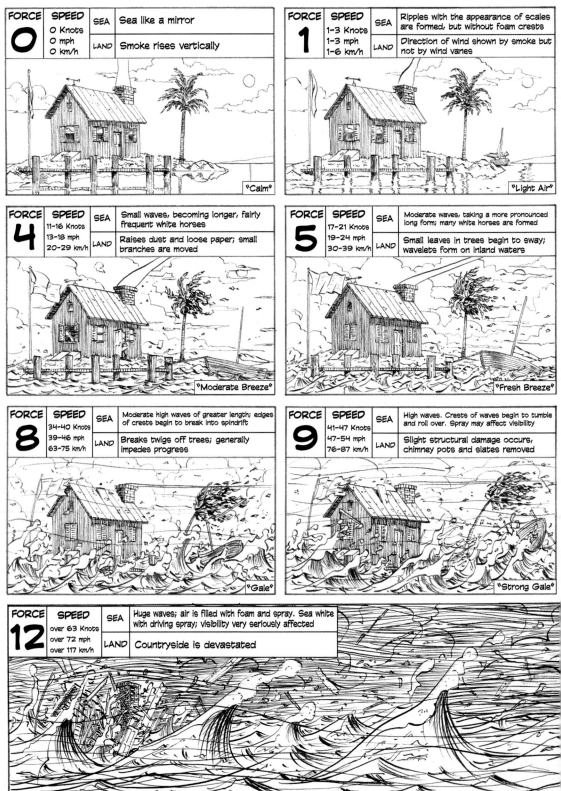

FORCE	SPEED		SEA/LAND	
0	0 Knots 0 mph 0 km/h		SEA	Sea like a mirror
			LAND	Smoke rises vertically

"Calm"

FORCE	SPEED		SEA/LAND	
1	1-3 Knots 1-3 mph 1-6 km/h		SEA	Ripples with the appearance of scales are formed, but without foam crests
			LAND	Direction of wind shown by smoke but not by wind vanes

"Light Air"

FORCE	SPEED		SEA/LAND	
4	11-16 Knots 13-18 mph 20-29 km/h		SEA	Small waves, becoming longer, fairly frequent white horses
			LAND	Raises dust and loose paper; small branches are moved

"Moderate Breeze"

FORCE	SPEED		SEA/LAND	
5	17-21 Knots 19-24 mph 30-39 km/h		SEA	Moderate waves, taking a more pronounced long form; many white horses are formed
			LAND	Small leaves in trees begin to sway; wavelets form on inland waters

"Fresh Breeze"

FORCE	SPEED		SEA/LAND	
8	34-40 Knots 39-46 mph 63-75 km/h		SEA	Moderate high waves of greater length; edges of crests begin to break into spindrift
			LAND	Breaks twigs off trees; generally impedes progress

"Gale"

FORCE	SPEED		SEA/LAND	
9	41-47 Knots 47-54 mph 76-87 km/h		SEA	High waves. Crests of waves begin to tumble and roll over. Spray may affect visibility
			LAND	Slight structural damage occurs, chimney pots and slates removed

"Strong Gale"

FORCE	SPEED		SEA/LAND	
12	over 63 Knots over 72 mph over 117 km/h		SEA	Huge waves; air is filled with foam and spray. Sea white with driving spray; visibility very seriously affected
			LAND	Countryside is devastated

Over thousands of years, sailors have learnt to estimate the speed of the wind just by looking about. In 1805, Francis Beaufort codified sailor's observations into what is now known as the Beaufort Scale. The universe tells you everything you need to know about it as long as you are prepared to watch, to listen, to smell, in short to observe.

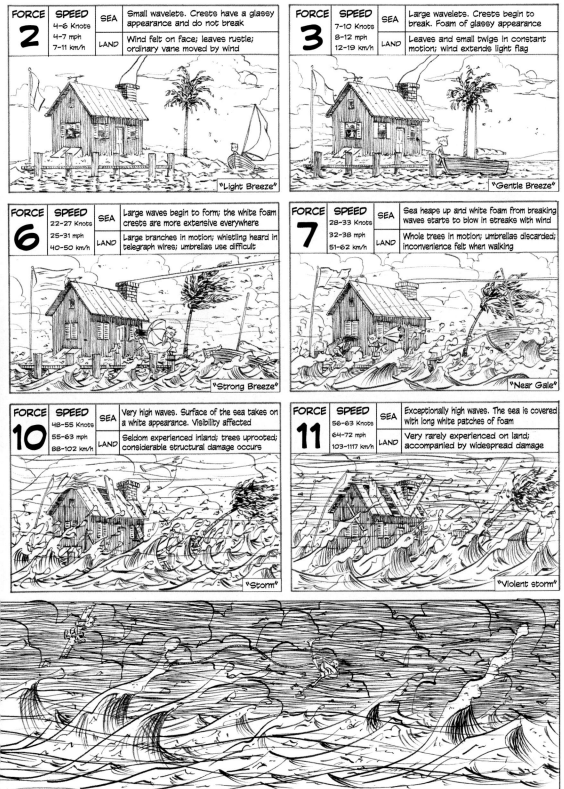

FORCE	SPEED	SEA	Small wavelets. Crests have a glassy appearance and do not break
2	4-6 Knots 4-7 mph 7-11 km/h	LAND	Wind felt on face; leaves rustle; ordinary vane moved by wind

"Light Breeze"

FORCE	SPEED	SEA	Large wavelets. Crests begin to break. Foam of glassy appearance
3	7-10 Knots 8-12 mph 12-19 km/h	LAND	Leaves and small twigs in constant motion; wind extends light flag

"Gentle Breeze"

FORCE	SPEED	SEA	Large waves begin to form; the white foam crests are more extensive everywhere
6	22-27 Knots 25-31 mph 40-50 km/h	LAND	Large branches in motion; whistling heard in telegraph wires; umbrellas use difficult

"Strong Breeze"

FORCE	SPEED	SEA	Sea heaps up and white foam from breaking waves starts to blow in streaks with wind
7	28-33 Knots 32-38 mph 51-62 km/h	LAND	Whole trees in motion; umbrellas discarded; inconvenience felt when walking

"Near Gale"

FORCE	SPEED	SEA	Very high waves. Surface of the sea takes on a white appearance. Visibility affected
10	48-55 Knots 55-63 mph 88-102 km/h	LAND	Seldom experienced inland; trees uprooted; considerable structural damage occurs

"Storm"

FORCE	SPEED	SEA	Exceptionally high waves. The sea is covered with long white patches of foam
11	56-63 Knots 64-72 mph 103-1117 km/h	LAND	Very rarely experienced on land; accompanied by widespread damage

"Violent storm"

"A SAILOR IS AN ARTIST WHOSE MEDIUM IS THE WIND."
— WEBB CHILES

HOWTOONS
CD HOVERCRAFT

MATERIALS:

BALLOON: FILLED WITH AIR, THIS IS YOUR BATTERY.

NOZZLE: THIS IS YOUR VALVE FOR CONTROLLING THE FLOW OF AIR.

FREE VALVE! ALWAYS BE ON THE LOOKOUT FOR USEFUL PROJECT PARTS IN EVERYDAY OBJECTS.

GLUE: HOLDS EVERYTHING TOGETHER.

CD: THIS IS YOUR HOVER-CRAFT BODY.

PLACE **BALLOON** OVER THE **NOZZLE**

GLUE **NOZZLE** TO **CD**

THE ELASTIC BALLOON *SLOWLY* RELEASES *PRESSURIZED AIR* UNDER THE CD.

THIS AIR ACTS AS A *CUSHION, FLOATING* THE HOVERCRAFT A HAIR'S WIDTH *ABOVE* THE TABLE.

BECAUSE THERE IS *NO CONTACT* BETWEEN THE CD AND THE SURFACE, THERE IS ALMOST *NO FRICTION* AND THE HOVERCRAFT CAN *GLIDE* GRACEFULLY IN ANY DIRECTION.

BLOW IN AIR

TO CHARGE

UP YOUR

BATTERY (BALLOON)

ON

OPEN VALVE

OFF

CLOSED VALVE

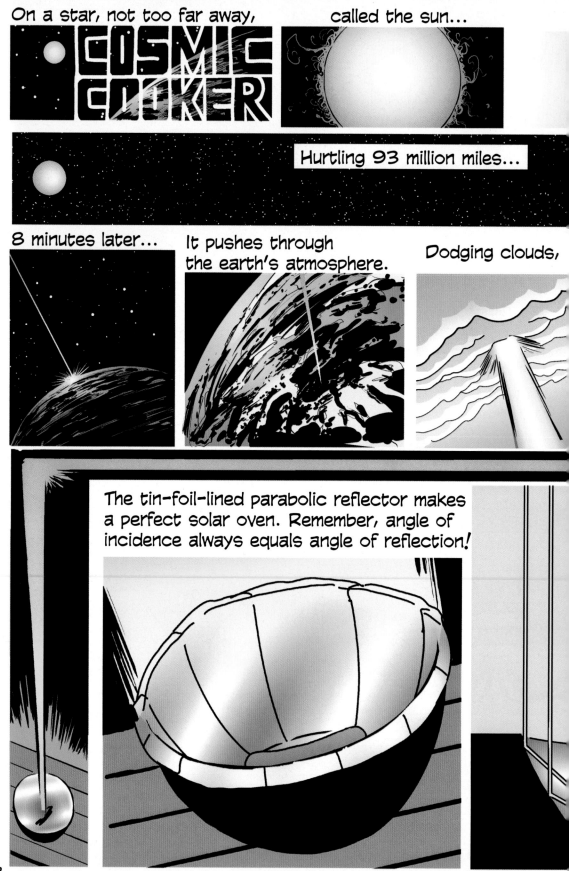

On a star, not too far away, called the sun...

COSMIC COOKER!

Hurtling 93 million miles...

8 minutes later...

It pushes through the earth's atmosphere.

Dodging clouds,

The tin-foil-lined parabolic reflector makes a perfect solar oven. Remember, angle of incidence always equals angle of reflection!

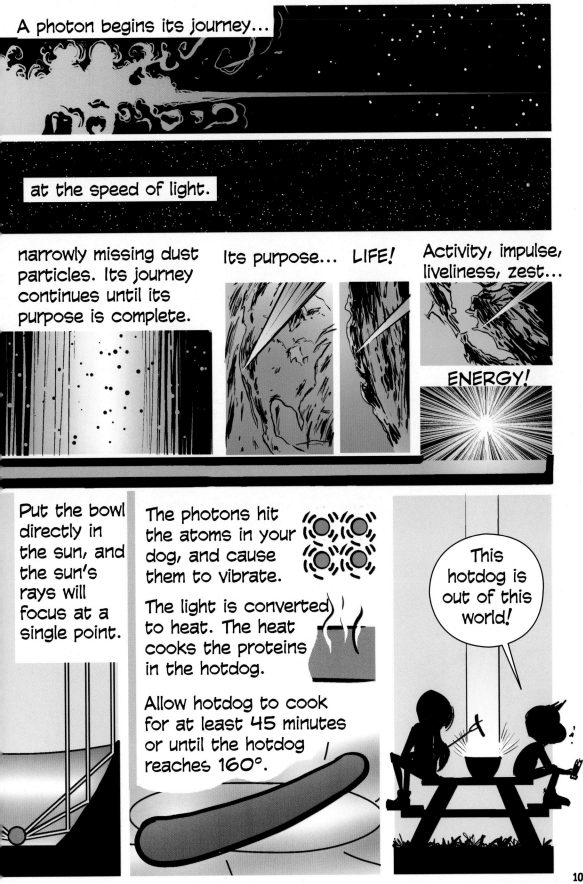

A photon begins its journey...

at the speed of light.

narrowly missing dust particles. Its journey continues until its purpose is complete.

Its purpose... LIFE!

Activity, impulse, liveliness, zest...

ENERGY!

Put the bowl directly in the sun, and the sun's rays will focus at a single point.

The photons hit the atoms in your dog, and cause them to vibrate.

The light is converted to heat. The heat cooks the proteins in the hotdog.

Allow hotdog to cook for at least 45 minutes or until the hotdog reaches 160°.

This hotdog is out of this world!

MAKE A RIPCORD ROTOR CHOPPER

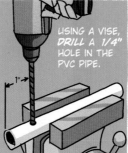

MATERIALS:

- SPONGE EMERY BOARD
- 7" WOODEN DOWEL
- 3 FT. KITE STRING
- 1/2" PVC PIPE CUT 6" LONG

USING A VISE, **DRILL A 1/4"** HOLE IN THE PVC PIPE.

DRILL A **3/32"** HOLE IN THE WOODEN DOWEL.

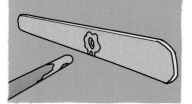

CUT A HOLE THROUGH THE EMERY BOARD AND GLUE THE WOODEN DOWEL TO THE BOARD.

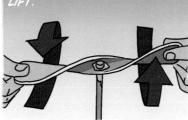

LET THE GLUE DRY. **TWIST** THE EMERY BOARD TO GIVE THE ROTOR **LIFT.**

THREAD THE STRING THROUGH THE PVC PIPE AND WOODEN DOWEL LIKE SO.

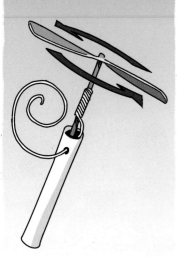

SPIN THE ROTOR **COUNTER-CLOCKWISE** TO WIND THE STRING AROUND THE DOWEL.

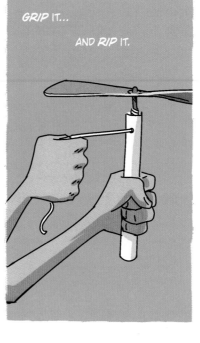

GRIP IT...

AND *RIP* IT.

GIVE IT A **WHIRL!**

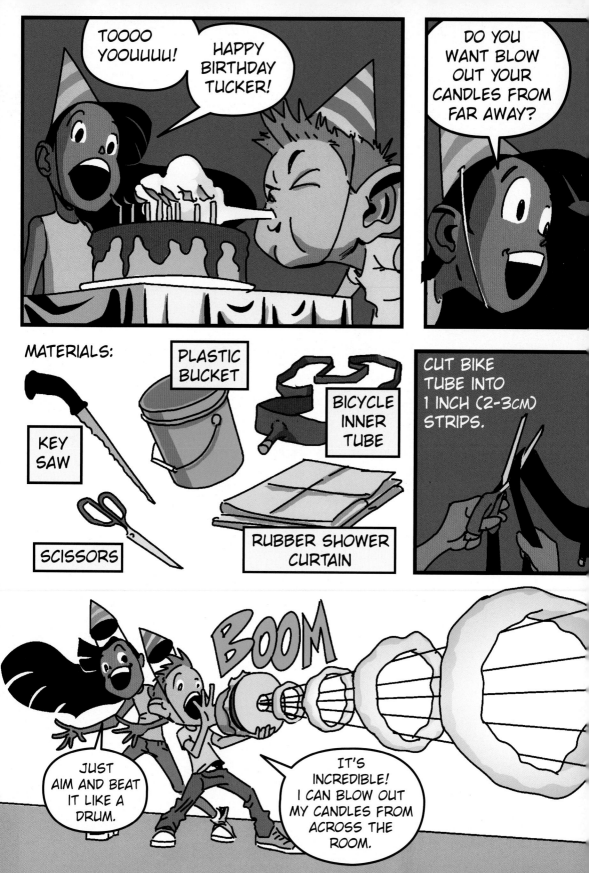

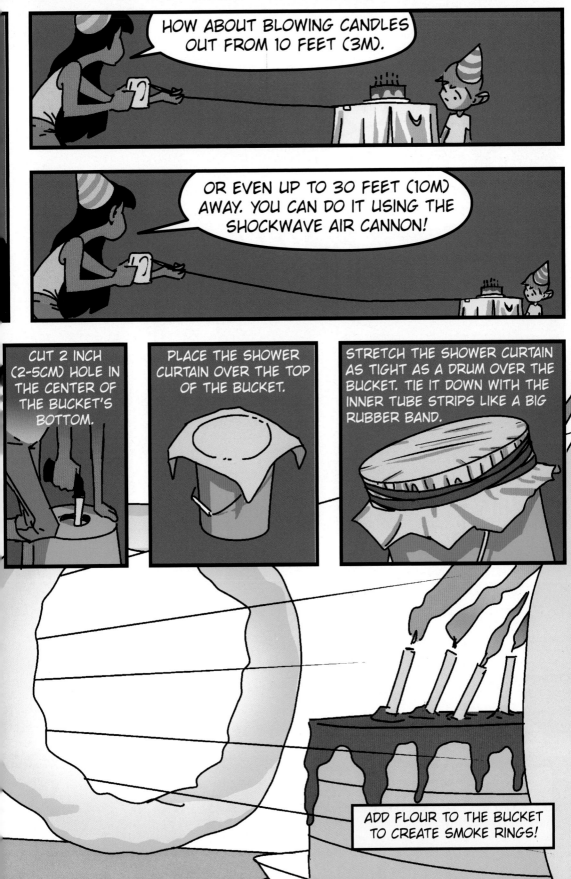

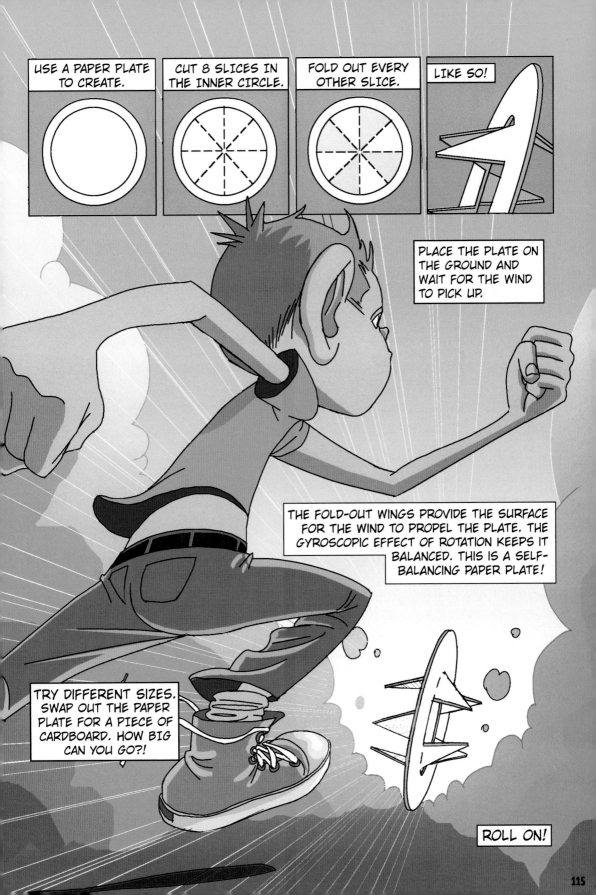

USE A PAPER PLATE TO CREATE.

CUT 8 SLICES IN THE INNER CIRCLE.

FOLD OUT EVERY OTHER SLICE.

LIKE SO!

PLACE THE PLATE ON THE GROUND AND WAIT FOR THE WIND TO PICK UP.

THE FOLD-OUT WINGS PROVIDE THE SURFACE FOR THE WIND TO PROPEL THE PLATE. THE GYROSCOPIC EFFECT OF ROTATION KEEPS IT BALANCED. THIS IS A SELF-BALANCING PAPER PLATE!

TRY DIFFERENT SIZES. SWAP OUT THE PAPER PLATE FOR A PIECE OF CARDBOARD. HOW BIG CAN YOU GO?!

ROLL ON!

115

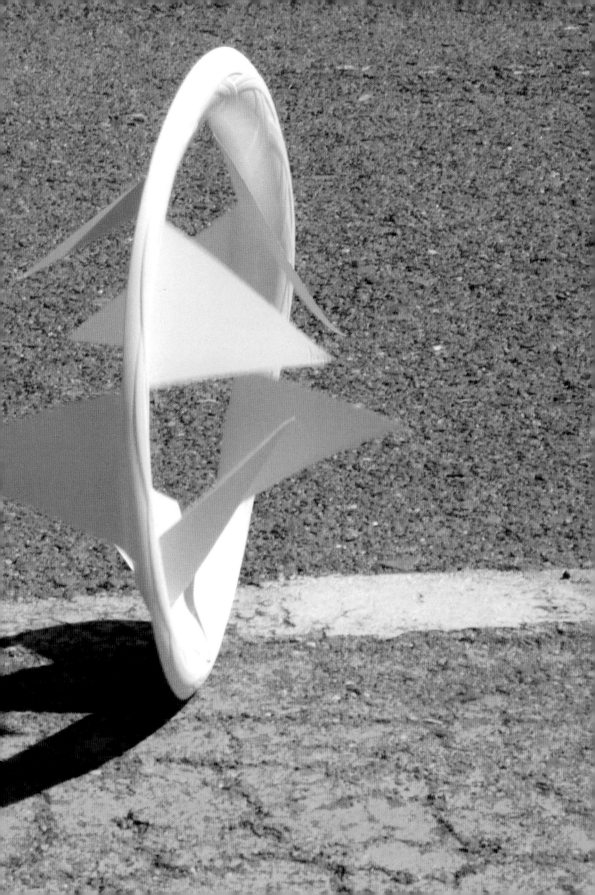

"ART IS EITHER PLAGIARISM
OR REVOLUTION."
- MARCEL DUCHAMP

ARTS & CRAFTS

There's so much technology around us that we sometimes forget about art, and its cousin, craft. Everybody benefits from the basic skills of art: drawing to communicate, drawing for pleasure, drawing for documentation. Being able to draw isn't just about putting a picture on a wall; it can help even the thorniest science project. Sometimes we need to draw something that a photograph can't capture, whether because it doesn't exist yet, or because by drawing things we can highlight important details. Not to mention that a pencil and paper are one of the most portable technologies around!

Crafting something to enjoy with simple materials is a lot of fun, whether it's a musical instrument, a piece of clothing, or a pinhole camera! If you learn to draw, you can create a fantastical costume. If you learn to craft, you can make it.

TURKEY BASTER FLUTE
PAGE 122

KALEIDO-SCOPE
PAGE 130

CAMERA OBSCURA
PAGE 131

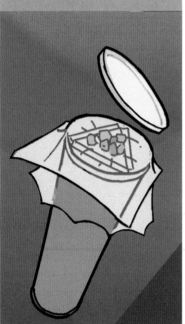

EXPRESS YOURSELF
PAGE 132

LET'S TALK ABOUT CHALK
PAGE 134

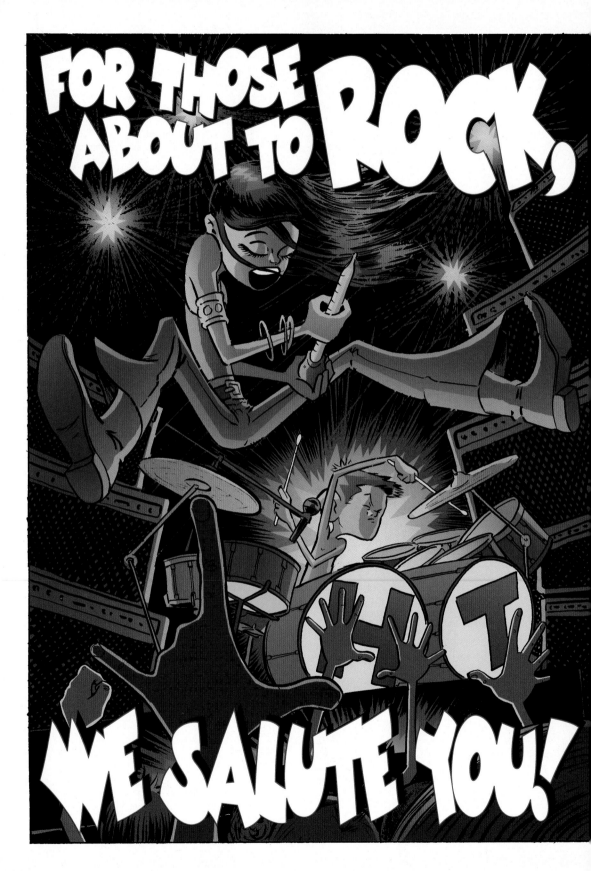

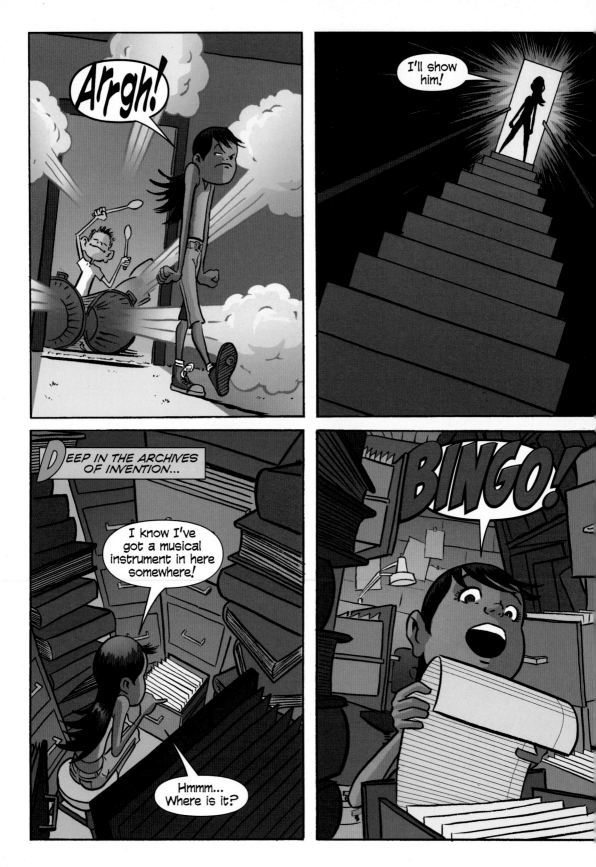

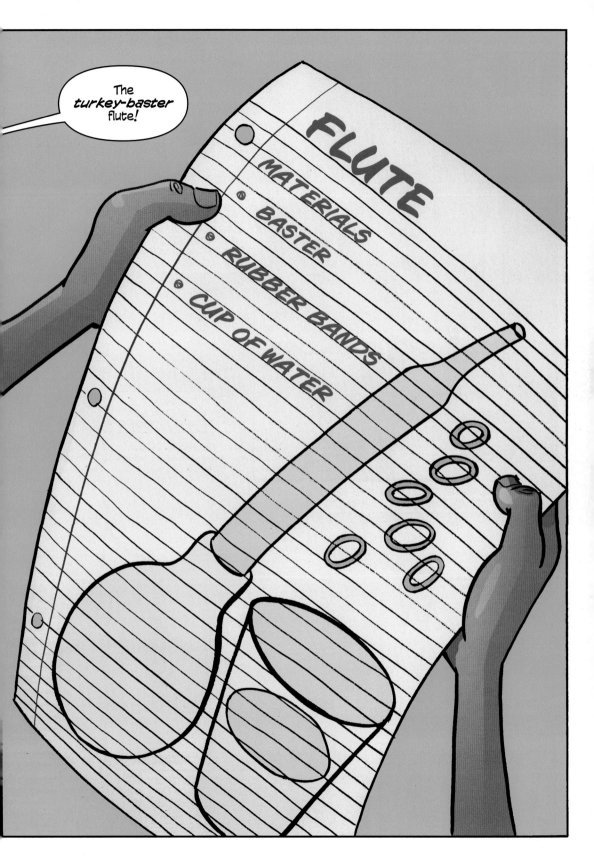

129

HOW TO DRAW CARTOON KALEIDOSCOPE

EIDOS = FORM

KALOS = BEAUTY

SKOPEO = TO LOOK

1 CAREFULLY *PUNCTURE* BOTTOM WITH SCREWDRIVER.

2 *CUT* FOAM CORE OR CARDBOARD TO 9" X 6.75" AND *SCORE* INTO THIRDS.

3 *GLUE* MYLAR SHEET TO THE *INSIDE*.

4 *FOLD* AND *TAPE* INTO A TRIANGLE.

5 *SLIDE* INTO CANISTER.

6 DRAPE *TRANSPARENT* PLASTIC WRAP INTO THE CANISTER.

7 *FILL* WITH LARGE BEADS.

8 COVER WITH *TRANSLUCENT* WAX PAPER.

9 *SECURE* WITH CAP AND *TRIM* EDGES.

MATERIALS

- PRINGLES CANISTER
- FOAM CORE OR CARDBOARD
- PLASTIC WRAP
- MYLAR PAPER
- WAX PAPER
- DUCT TAPE
- BEADS
- GLUE

WOW!

SPIN THE CANISTER TO *SEE* THE *BEAUTIFUL SHAPES* AND COLORS!

HOWTOONS: CAMERA OBSCURA

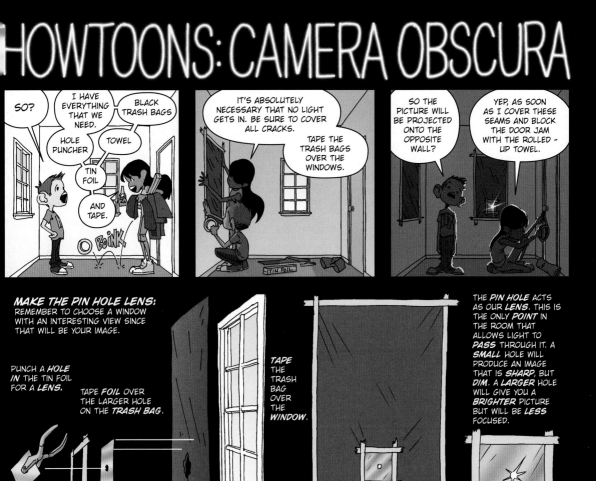

MAKE THE PIN HOLE LENS:
REMEMBER TO CHOOSE A WINDOW WITH AN INTERESTING VIEW SINCE THAT WILL BE YOUR IMAGE.

PUNCH A *HOLE IN* THE TIN FOIL FOR A *LENS.*

TAPE *FOIL* OVER THE LARGER HOLE ON THE *TRASH BAG.*

TAPE THE TRASH BAG OVER THE *WINDOW.*

THE *PIN HOLE* ACTS AS OUR *LENS.* THIS IS THE ONLY *POINT* IN THE ROOM THAT ALLOWS LIGHT TO *PASS* THROUGH IT. A *SMALL* HOLE WILL PRODUCE AN IMAGE THAT IS *SHARP,* BUT *DIM.* A *LARGER* HOLE WILL GIVE YOU A *BRIGHTER* PICTURE BUT WILL BE *LESS* FOCUSED.

IMAGES APPEAR *UPSIDE DOWN* BECAUSE WHEN THE SUN SHINES, *LIGHT RAYS* TRAVEL DOWN TO EARTH AND BOUNCE OFF THAT TREE. BEING THAT LIGHT ALWAYS TRAVELS IN *STRAIGHT LINES,* THAT LIGHT RAY WILL *BOUNCE* OFF AT AN *ANGLE.* OUR TIN FOIL PIN HOLE CATCHES THAT REFLECTED RAY AND PROJECTS IT ONTO THE WALL UPSIDE DOWN. THIS IS HOW ALL REFLECTED LIGHT IS *VIEWED*; OUR BRAINS *FLIP* THE IMAGE FOR US.

CREATE YOUR OWN T-SHIRT DESIGNS WITH EASE. USE A WAX CRAYON AND DRAW DIRECTLY ON A T-SHIRT. WHITE TEES WORK BEST. GET CREATIVE!

ALWAYS GET AN ADULT WHEN IRONING! TO SATURATE YOUR DESIGN INTO THE SHIRT YOU'LL NEED THAT ADULT TO IRON.

THANKS FOR THE *HELP!*

LAYER A PIECE OF WAX PAPER AND A PILLOW CASE OVER THE DESIGN BEFORE IRONING.

IRON

YOU CAN WASH YOUR SHIRT TO SET THE COLORS AND PREVENT ANY BLEEDING.

PILLOW CASE

DESIGN FOR THE RUNWAY YOUR WAY!

WAX PAPER

CREATE LOGOS.

GET RETRO.

GO PUNK!

T-SHIRT

IRONING BOARD

THINK ABOUT THE CUT. YOUR STYLE IS ONLY LIMITED BY YOUR IMAGINATION.

MAKE A DRESS.

RIP IT UP.

OR GO SHORT.

EXPRESS YOURSELF!

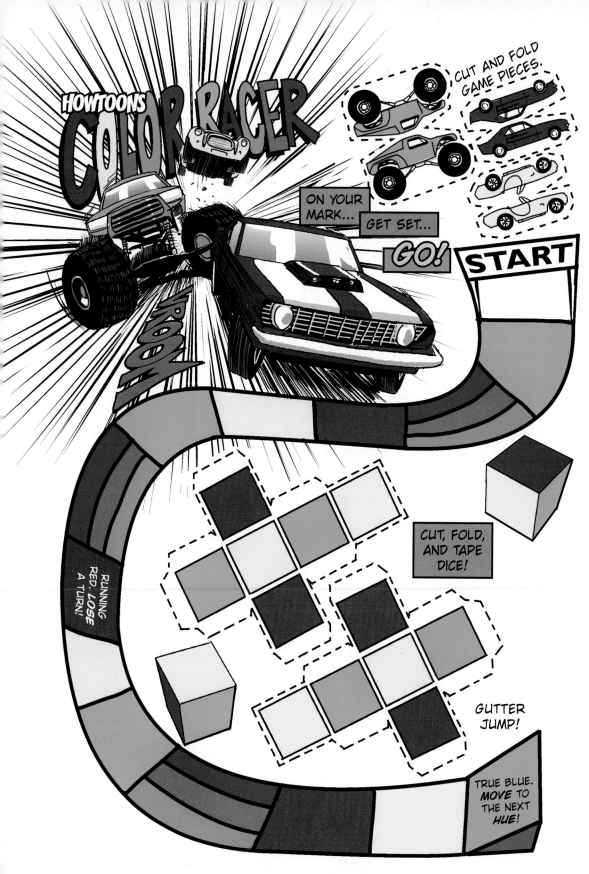

ROLL THE TWO DICE. IF YOU ROLL TWO OF THE SAME COLORS, MOVE TO THAT PRIMARY COLOR. IF TWO DIFFERENT COLORS COME UP, MOVE TO THAT SECONDARY COLOR. FIRST TO CROSS THE FINISH LINE WINS!

YELLOW
PRIMARY

ORANGE
SECONDARY

GREEN
SECONDARY

RED
PRIMARY

BLUE
PRIMARY

PURPLE
SECONDARY

FINISH!

YOU'RE DRIVING A REAL LEMON. GO BACK TO GUTTER JUMP!

DRAGOTTA '12

137

create creatures with your own stuffed animals!

pattern

trace pattern and a 1/4" border on the wrong side of the cloth.

x2

① place arms and feet along the inside of one layer

materials:

2 fabric bodies
1 felt stomach
2 felt arms
2 felt legs
decorative add ons

⑤ flip inside out

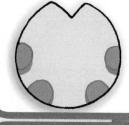

② overlay second layer

③ stitch along border

④ leave a 1"-1.5" opening

⑥ add stuffing

⑦ sew shut

⑧ decorate!

artwork by meredith mcclaren

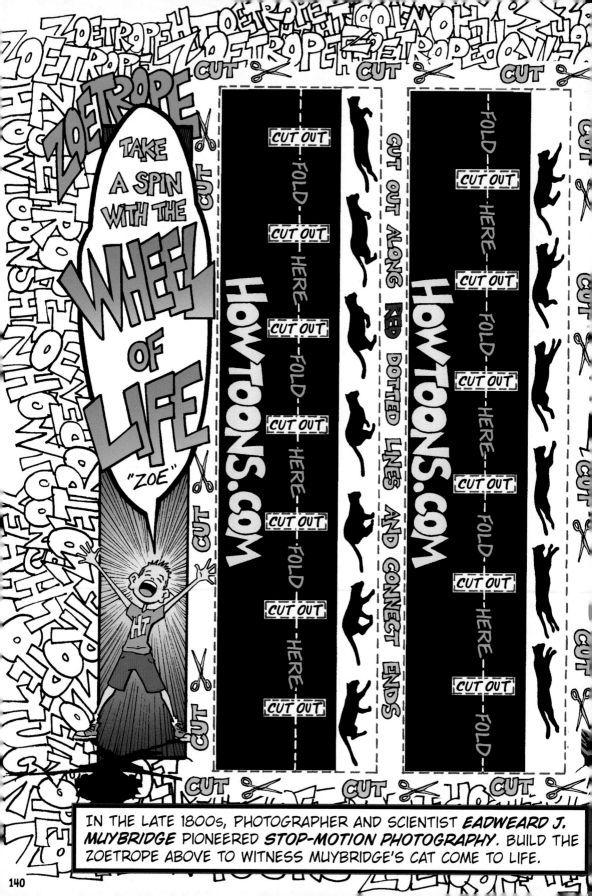

IN THE LATE 1800s, PHOTOGRAPHER AND SCIENTIST *EADWEARD J. MUYBRIDGE* PIONEERED *STOP-MOTION PHOTOGRAPHY*. BUILD THE ZOETROPE ABOVE TO WITNESS MUYBRIDGE'S CAT COME TO LIFE.

PHOTOCOPY THE STRIPS.

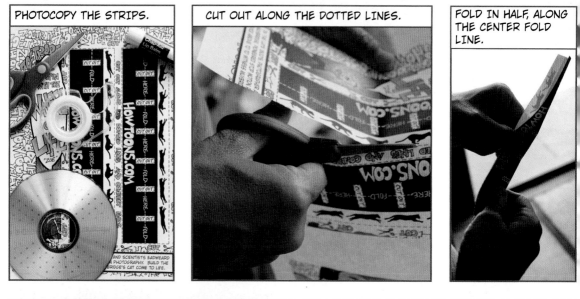

CUT OUT ALONG THE DOTTED LINES.

FOLD IN HALF, ALONG THE CENTER FOLD LINE.

CUT OUT THE SMALL SLITS IN THE FOLDED STRIPS TO CREATE PERSISTENCE OF VISION.

ATTACH STRIPS, OVERLAPPING THE TABS. ALIGN THE CORRECT CATS.

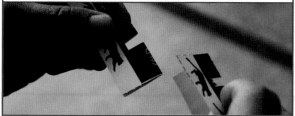

TAPE ONE SIDE...

THEN THE OTHER.

CENTER LOOPED STRIP ON TOP OF THE CD AND TAPE IT DOWN.

USE THE CHAPSTICK AS YOUR AXLE. CLOSE CAP TO FASTEN.

SPIN THE CD AND LOOK THROUGH THE SLITS TO THE CAT ON THE INSIDE. LOOKING THROUGH THE SLITS CREATES THE PHENOMENON KNOWN AS *PERSISTENCE OF VISION*.

SPECIAL THANKS TO *VICKY* AND *GARRETT!*

LAID OUT LIKE SO, ALL *I* HAD *TO DO* WAS *EXECUTE.*

BEING WELL *PREPARED*, I WAS *CONFIDENT*. SUCCESS WAS A MATTER OF PATIENCE AND FOCUS.

I MADE THE CUTS *CAREFULLY*, THE FOLDS *PRECISELY*.

WITH CONFIDENCE I COULD NOW *IMPROVISE*. I MADE SLEEVES AND *TAPED* THE SEAMS SHUT WITH *DUCT TAPE*.

THE COAT WAS A PERFECT FIT.

NOW, WALKING THE STREETS I *CONTEMPLATED* THE *POSSIBILITIES*.

ALL THE DIFFERENT COATS THAT WERE *WITHIN* MY REACH.

TRASH BAG RAIN COAT

DUCT-TAPE SEAMS

WHERE *OTHERS* HAD SEEN ONLY TRASH BAGS,

RECEPTACLES *FIT* ONLY TO RECEIVE OUR *WASTE*,

I HAD SEEN SOMETHING DIFFERENT...

AND *IT* WAS BEAUTIFUL IN ITS SIMPLE *FUNCTION*.

CUT SLITS AND STRIPS FOR BELT.

THE *RAIN* LIGHTLY MASSAGED MY BRAIN.

IT WOULD BE *IMPERVIOUS* TO THE ELEMENTS THAT WOULD *IMPRISON* ME.

I WAS FREE.

DRAGOTTA, GRIFFITH, BONSEN

APOLOGIES TO *FRANK MILLER!*

147

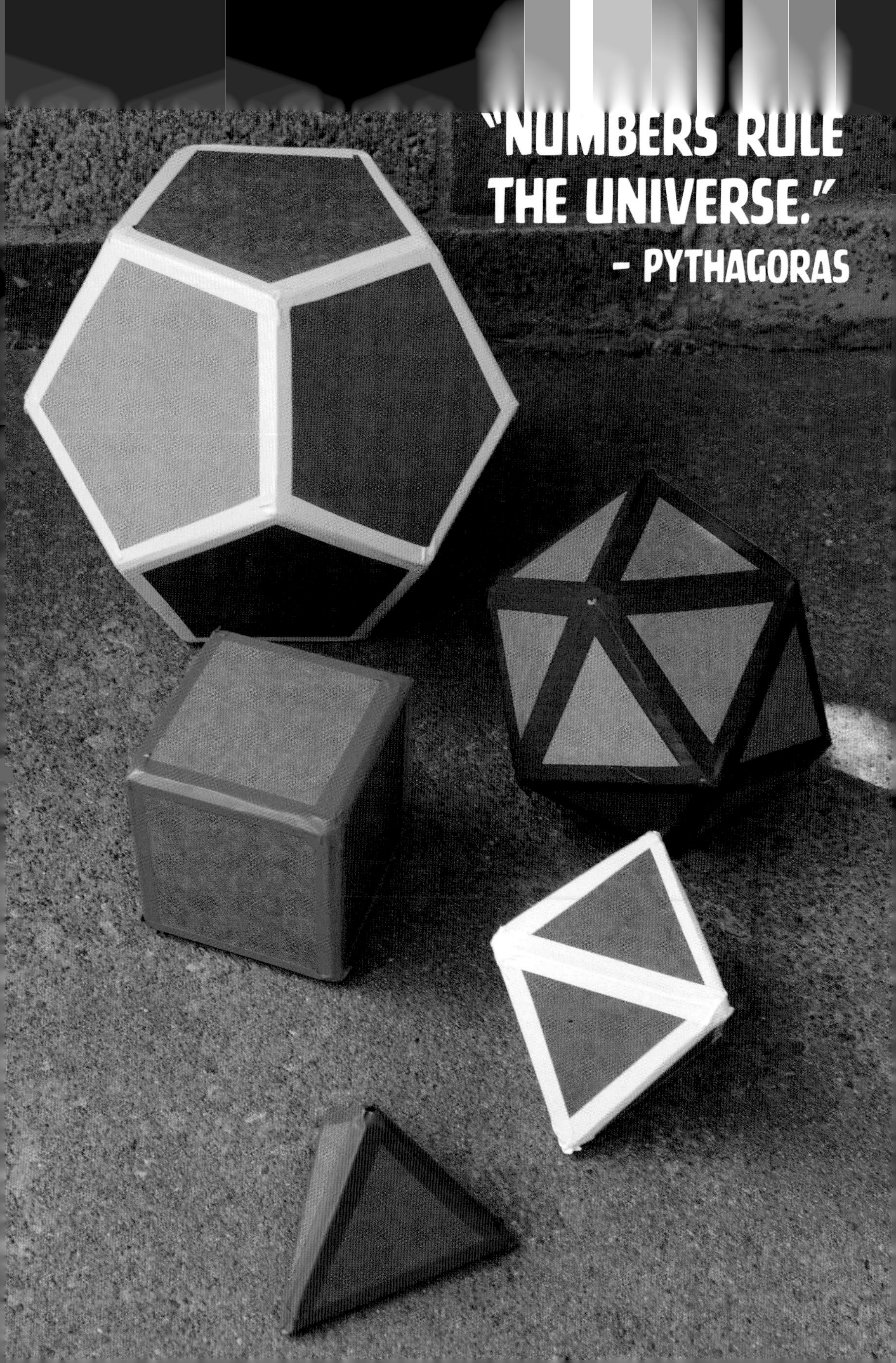
"NUMBERS RULE THE UNIVERSE."
- PYTHAGORAS

MATH & GEOMETRY

Far from being abstract, far from being useless, math is infused in everything. It surrounds us. Math is the language that enables the rest of the sciences to describe the universe, from the simple counting of things, to manipulating the equations of motion, to developing new methods of computing. But to think of math as just a way to count is to fall way short of what math can be. Math, just like art, poetry, and music, is deliciously complex and varied. You may not like a particular song or painting, but that doesn't mean you don't like music or art! So too with math: there's a beautiful piece of mathematics or geometry out there for everyone, waiting to be enjoyed and loved, because it is beautiful. The fun of origami, the joy of games like Sudoku, the elegant geometry of architecture, the proportions of humans and animals, the joyful stacking of bricks, polyhedra, and Legos, shapes and patterns in the tiles on the bathroom floor … all pieces of math that can be enjoyed as art, as puzzle, and as play.

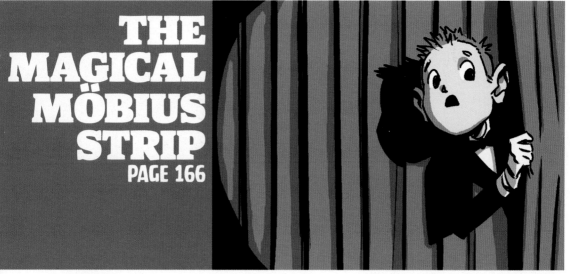

817
818

819
820

What's this crazy sign language you're flipping, Tuck?

Shh, I'm not signing, I'm counting my comics.

I've got to keep concentrating.

You still use your fingers to count? I thought you were past that, Tuck.

I'm *so* past that. I'm into counting in binary now. It's awesome. I have the capacity to count like a computer.

With a single hand I can count to 31; with two I can reach 1023! Enough even for my monster comic collection.

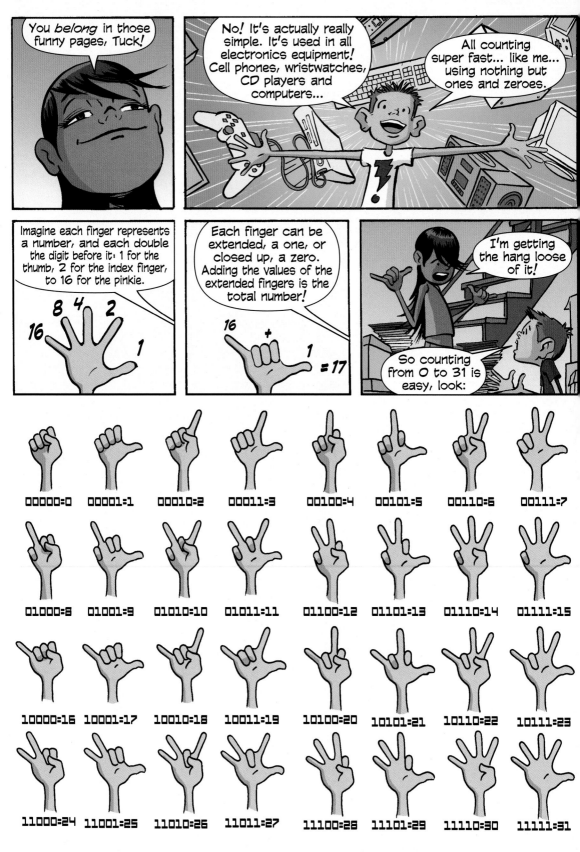

Then to get to 1023, I simply add my next 5 fingers ... 32, 64, 128, 256, 512.

I can even go over a million when I use my toes. 1,048,575 to be precise ...

That stinks, Tuck.

No not at all, this binary counting system is what makes everything work.

Robots...

...computers...

...and telecommunications through wires or fiber optics.

In electronics, the zeros and ones are represented by high and low voltages, or flashes of lights, not by my fingers... A zero or a one is called a bit.

It's all a bit hard to believe, Tuck! Get it? Bit hard ...!

Only if you byte off more than you can chew!

The End!

GEORGE E. BROKE
THE TWELVE FACES

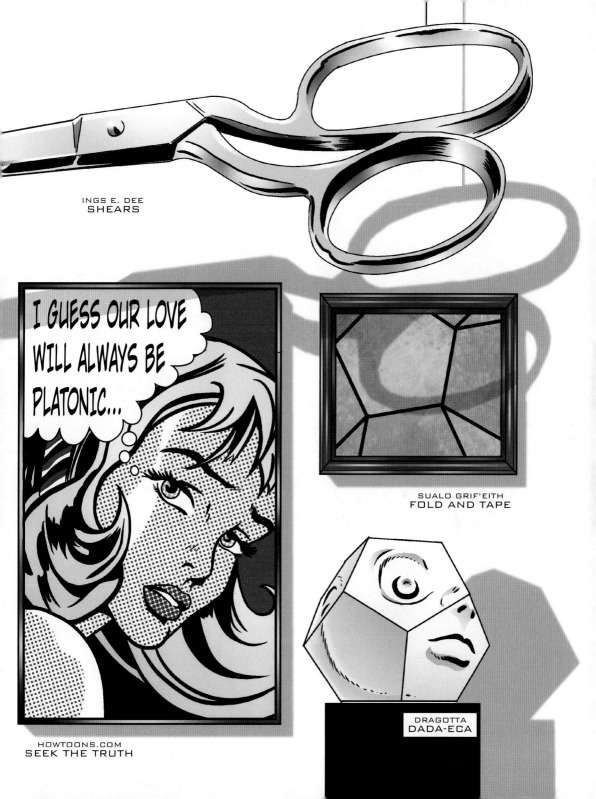

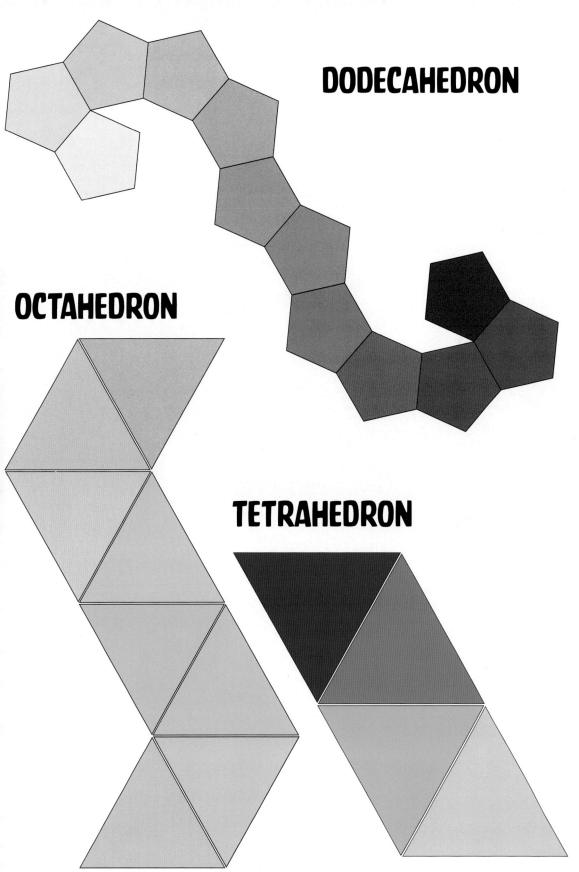

DODECAHEDRON

OCTAHEDRON

TETRAHEDRON

161

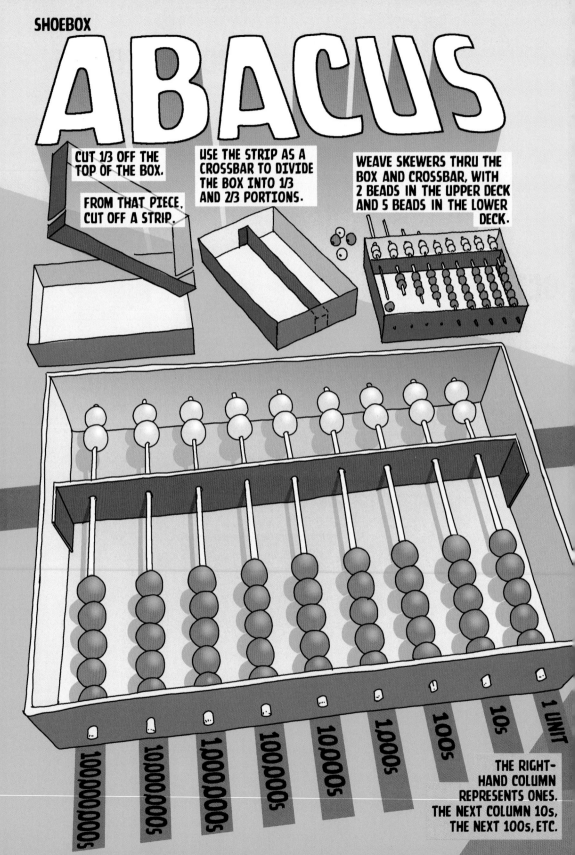

SHOEBOX ABACUS

CUT 1/3 OFF THE TOP OF THE BOX.

FROM THAT PIECE, CUT OFF A STRIP.

USE THE STRIP AS A CROSSBAR TO DIVIDE THE BOX INTO 1/3 AND 2/3 PORTIONS.

WEAVE SKEWERS THRU THE BOX AND CROSSBAR, WITH 2 BEADS IN THE UPPER DECK AND 5 BEADS IN THE LOWER DECK.

100,000,000s
10,000,000s
1,000,000s
100,000s
10,000s
1,000s
100s
10s
1 UNIT

THE RIGHT-HAND COLUMN REPRESENTS ONES. THE NEXT COLUMN 10s, THE NEXT 100s, ETC.

LONG BEFORE WRITTEN NUMBERS EXISTED, THE ABACUS WAS INVENTED AS A TOOL TO HELP MERCHANTS COUNT LARGE NUMBERS AND CALCULATE THE COST OF GOODS. THE ABACUS IS STILL WIDELY USED TODAY.

EACH BEAD IN THE UPPER DECK HAS A VALUE OF 5.

BEADS ARE CONSIDERED COUNTED WHEN MOVED TO THE CROSSBAR.

EACH BEAD IN THE LOWER DECK HAS A VALUE OF ONE.

AFTER 5 BEADS ARE COUNTED IN THE LOWER DECK, THE RESULT IS CARRIED TO THE UPPER DECK.

IF BOTH BEADS IN THE UPPER DECK ARE COUNTED THE RESULT IS THEN CARRIED TO THE LEFT-HAND COLUMN.

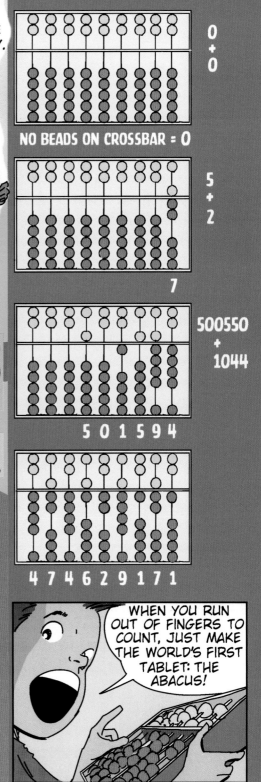

NO BEADS ON CROSSBAR = 0

0 + 0

5 + 2

7

500550 + 1044

5 0 1 5 9 4

4 7 4 6 2 9 1 7 1

WHEN YOU RUN OUT OF FINGERS TO COUNT, JUST MAKE THE WORLD'S FIRST TABLET: THE ABACUS!

THE MEASURE OF MIGHT

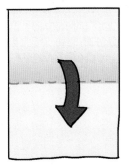

USING THESE **6 GEOMETRIC FOLDS** WE CAN MAKE THIS SHEET **MEASURE** ANYTHING IN **INCHES.**

11/2=5.5

8.5-5.5=3

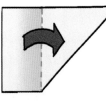

5.5-3=2.5

3-2.5=.5

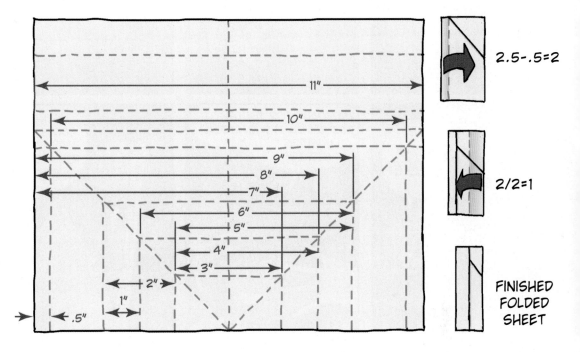

11"

10"

9"

8"

7"

6"

5"

4"

3"

2"

1"

.5"

2.5-.5=2

2/2=1

FINISHED
FOLDED
SHEET

GEOMETRY ENLIGHT-ENS THE INTELLECT AND SETS ONE'S MIND RIGHT. ALL ITS PROOFS ARE VERY CLEAR AND ORDERLY. IT IS HARDLY POSSIBLE FOR ERRORS TO ENTER INTO GEO-METRICAL REASONING, BECAUSE IT IS WELL ARRANGED AND ORDERLY. THUS, THE MIND THAT CONSTANTLY APPLIES ITSELF TO GEOMETRY IS NOT LIKELY TO FALL INTO ERROR.

—IBN KHALDUN, 1332-1406

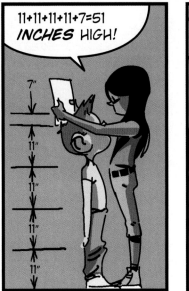

11+11+11+11+7=51
INCHES HIGH!

7"

11"

11"

11"

11"

11"

THAT'S
4'3"
SHORTY!

WOW!
GEOMETRY
CAN EVEN BE
USED FOR
COMEDY.

THE MAGICAL
MÖBIUS
STRIP!

UM...

HEY... PSSST... *CELINE* WE'RE ON.

GOOD EVENING! *I* AM *TUCKER* THE PECULIAR. *COADJUTANT* TO...

THE *GREAT CELINIE!*

BEHOLD! FOR TONIGHT I BRING YOU THE MYSTICAL *MÖBIUS STRIP!*

AHEM... *TUCKER* THE PAPER PLEASE!

USING AN ORDINARY NEWSPAPER, RIP A 3-INCH STRIP!

TUCKER! CAN YOU ATTEST THAT IT IS JUST REGULAR PULP?

I CAN!

NOW IF YOU WILL, CAN YOU PLEASE *TWIST* ONE END OVER AND CONNECT IT TO THE OTHER *SIDE* USING TAPE?

WITNESS LADIES AND GENTLEMEN, THE CURIOUS *MÖBIUS* STRIP!

IT IS CHIRAL, A SURFACE WITH ONLY ONE SIDE, AND ONE BOUNDARY!

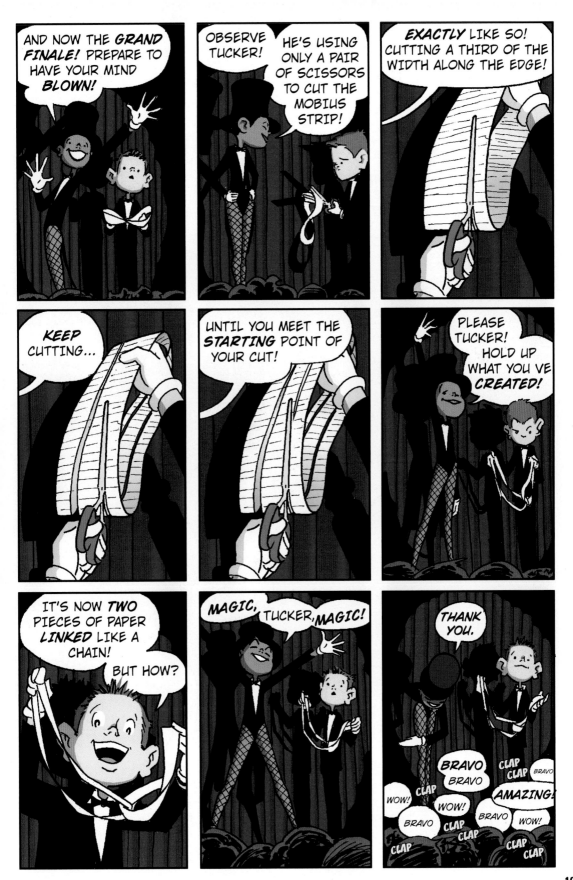

GAMI-BOT

ROBOTS ARE SMART MACHINES CAPABLE OF AUTONO-MOUSLY PRODUCING COMPLEX MOTION TO PERFORM COORDINATED TASKS LIKE RUNNING. THEY ARE USUALLY ELECTRO-MECHANICAL IN NATURE AND ARE GUIDED BY INTELLIGENCE EMBEDDED IN MECHANISMS, ELECTRONIC CIRCUITS OR COMPUTER PROGRAMMING. BUT NOT ALWAYS!

IT'S THAT **EASY** TO MAKE A **ROBOT.**

YEP, IT ALMOST **BUILDS** ITSELF!

FOAM TAPE

TAPE

VIBRATION MOTOR

3V CELL BATTERY

Business Card
14 Re-Use Lane
Placetobe, Ca
·)1234

BUSINESS CARD

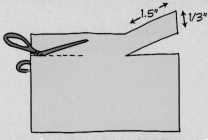

1 CUT 2 STRIPS 1.5" FROM EACH SIDE 1/3" DOWN

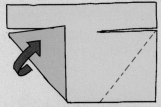

2 VALLEY-FOLD CORNERS UP TO MEET CUT LINES CREATING A VALLEY CREASE.

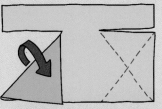

3 VALLEY-FOLD TOP CORNER DOWN CREATING A DIAGONAL.

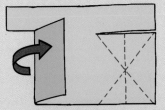

4 FOLD IN HALF ALONG THE CREASE AND TURN OVER AND REPEAT.

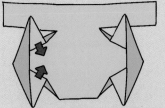

5 CREATE A COLLAPSABLE FOLD BY PINCHING THE CENTER CREASE IN.

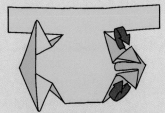

6 FOLD CORNER POINTS UPWARDS TO MAKE YOUR LEGS.

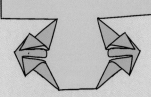

7 REPEAT WITH THE OTHER SIDE.

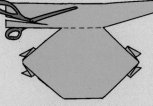

8 SHAPE YOUR ANTENNAS BY CUTTING DIAGONAL LINES.

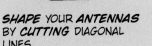

9 VALLEY-FOLD ANTENNA UP ALONG THE CUT LINES.

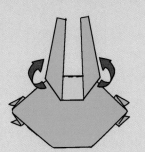

10 VALLEY-FOLD ANTENNAS UP.

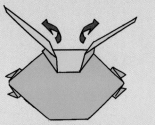

11 MOUNTAIN-FOLD ANTENNAS DOWN.

12 PUT IT TOGETHER!

TAPE

STRIP WIRE FROM VIBRATION MOTOR.

BATTERY

FOAM TAPE

HOWTOONS.COM

*PRESS DOWN ON THE GAMI-BOT TO EVEN THE SURFACE AREA OF LEGS AND HELP THE BOT GO STRAIGHT.

"A SCIENTIST IN HIS LABORATORY IS NOT A MERE TECHNICIAN: HE IS ALSO A CHILD CONFRONTING NATURAL PHENOMENA THAT IMPRESS HIM AS THOUGH THEY WERE FAIRY TALES."

- MARIE CURIE

SCIENCE

People argue over what science is and what its limits are all the time. Science is the discovery of the new. New creatures, new phenomena, new ways of describing things we experience. Science is adventure. Occasionally science is about reproducing results and doing things twice, but we can leave that to the grownups for now. In the short term, science can be purely for reasons of wonder. Reasons of why: Why do I sneeze? Why do things fall down, not up? Why do stars twinkle? Why are there clouds? All of those Whys are a lifetime of adventures, and each experiment helps you learn a little more about the universe we live in. Pick any one of them and you have an antidote to boredom for the rest of your life! Pick all of these Whys and you have a myriad of adventures and experiences waiting for you to pioneer and enjoy. You don't have to want to be a Scientist to be a scientist; even babies test the limits of physics by dropping food off their tray over, and over, and over again. Even something as simple as making your own ice cream is possible because long ago a scientist discovered that... well, you'll see.

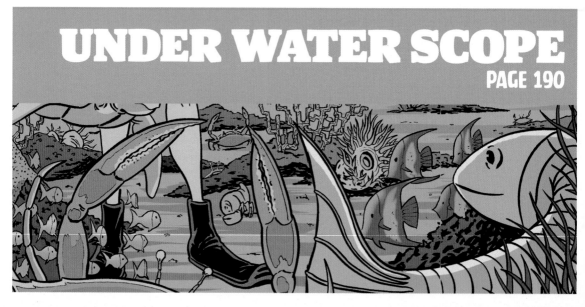

FROM THE **GLACIERS** OF NORWAY THEY CUT THE PUREST BLOCKS OF ICE, A **DELICACY** IN WARMER CLIMATES — THEY HAD TO MOVE **QUICKLY** WITH THEIR PRECIOUS QUARRY...

THEY FOUND **SUGAR** IN PERSIA, A VALUABLE COMMODITY THAT HAD MADE ITS WAY FROM **NEW GUINEA** VIA **INDIA** AND **CHINA**...

SUGAR

FROM **SPANISH** CONQUISTADORS THEY RECEIVED SOME OF THE FIRST SAMPLES OF THE VERSATILE **VANILLA BEAN** THAT WAS BEING CULTIVATED IN **MEXICO**.

IN NORTHERN EUROPE THEY FOUND THE **FRESHEST MILK** AND DIVINED THE **SECRETS** OF MAKING THE **THICKEST** CREAM!

A CLAY URN OF **SALT** CRACKED INTO THE HESSIAN SACK'S OF **ICE**.

THE POTS OF SUGAR, VANILLA BEAN, CREAM, MILK AND SPICES ALL BROKE INTO ANOTHER SADDLE BAG.

AND BY DIVINE FATE THAT **SADDLE BAG** FELL UPON THE OPEN SACK OF **SALT AND ICE!**

THE TWO GREAT EXPLORERS SAW THEIR INGREDIENTS **FREEZE** QUICKLY IN THE SALT AND ICE MIX.

Hey! All of the goods mixed up and made that giant mound of ice and cream.

With a *cherry* on top!

MANY OF THE WORLD'S GREATEST CREATIONS WERE BROUGHT ABOUT BY THE CAREFUL AND ENLIGHTENED OBSERVATION OF AN **ACCIDENT!**

Mmmm. Creamy-ice. *Smooth* and *delicious!*

The king *will* be pleased.

Provided you don't eat it all.

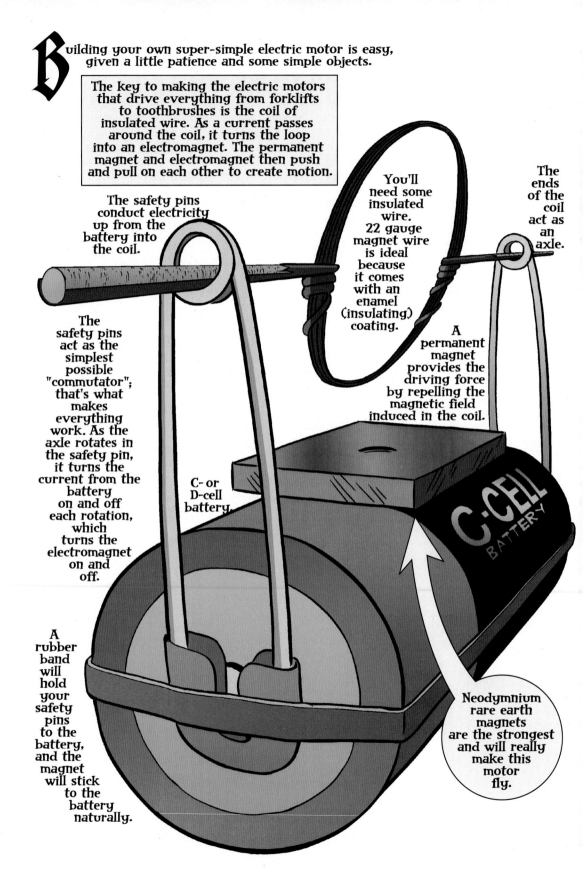

Building your own super-simple electric motor is easy, given a little patience and some simple objects.

The key to making the electric motors that drive everything from forklifts to toothbrushes is the coil of insulated wire. As a current passes around the coil, it turns the loop into an electromagnet. The permanent magnet and electromagnet then push and pull on each other to create motion.

The safety pins conduct electricity up from the battery into the coil.

You'll need some insulated wire. 22 gauge magnet wire is ideal because it comes with an enamel (insulating) coating.

The ends of the coil act as an axle.

The safety pins act as the simplest possible "commutator"; that's what makes everything work. As the axle rotates in the safety pin, it turns the current from the battery on and off each rotation, which turns the electromagnet on and off.

A permanent magnet provides the driving force by repelling the magnetic field induced in the coil.

C- or D-cell battery.

A rubber band will hold your safety pins to the battery, and the magnet will stick to the battery naturally.

Neodymnium rare earth magnets are the strongest and will really make this motor fly.

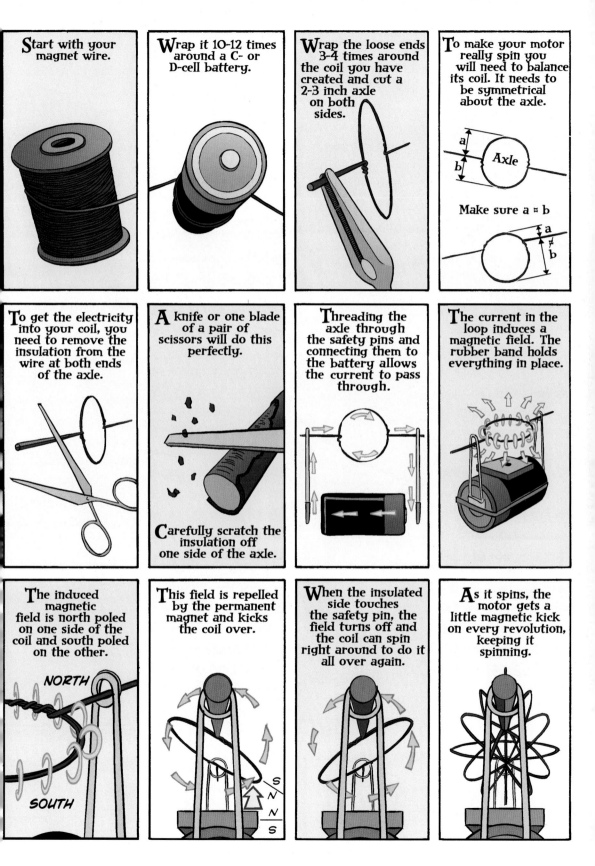

Start with your magnet wire.

Wrap it 10-12 times around a C- or D-cell battery.

Wrap the loose ends 3-4 times around the coil you have created and cut a 2-3 inch axle on both sides.

To make your motor really spin you will need to balance its coil. It needs to be symmetrical about the axle.

Axle

Make sure a ≠ b

To get the electricity into your coil, you need to remove the insulation from the wire at both ends of the axle.

A knife or one blade of a pair of scissors will do this perfectly.

Carefully scratch the insulation off one side of the axle.

Threading the axle through the safety pins and connecting them to the battery allows the current to pass through.

The current in the loop induces a magnetic field. The rubber band holds everything in place.

The induced magnetic field is north poled on one side of the coil and south poled on the other.

NORTH

SOUTH

This field is repelled by the permanent magnet and kicks the coil over.

When the insulated side touches the safety pin, the field turns off and the coil can spin right around to do it all over again.

As it spins, the motor gets a little magnetic kick on every revolution, keeping it spinning.

CAREFULLY CUT A 1/2" HOLE IN THE LOWER THIRD OF THE BOTTLE.

PUNCH OUT A HOLE IN A PIECE OF DUCT TAPE. ALIGN THE TWO HOLES AND STICK TAPE TO BOTTLE.

FIRST, POUR SEVERAL DROPS OF MILK INTO THE BOTTLE. THEN FILL WITH WATER. MIX SHOULD BE CLOUDY. PLUG HOLE WITH FINGER.

SCREW ON THE CAP OF BOTTLE AND REMOVE YOUR FINGER. THE WATER WILL STAY IN THE BOTTLE UNTIL MORE AIR IS LET IN THROUGH THE TOP.

TO GET A STEADY BEAM OF LIGHT USE A FLASH-LIGHT IN A BOX WITH PIN HOLE CUT IN IT. FOR OPTIMAL RESULTS, USE A LASER POINTER.

TWIST THE BOTTLE AND ALIGN THE BEAM SO IT SHINES THROUGH THE BOTTLE AND OUT THE HOLE.

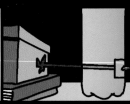

TERRARIUM

I'm going to need a spacecraft that can support human life for long periods of time without resupply ships...
And scientists haven't yet figured out how to create such a complex ecosystem. It's hard, like trying to make a miniature world...
And we humans haven't exactly figured out how not to pollute Earth, either...
So I'm practicing here in my...
TERRARIUM!

A NICE BIG PICKLE JAR WITH A LID WILL WORK NICELY. YOU COULD USE A FISH TANK, OR EVEN A LARGE SODA BOTTLE WITH THE TOP CUT OFF.

P LACE A FEW INCHES OF DIRT IN THE JAR, WITH PEBBLES ON THE BOTTOM TO GIVE IT BETTER DRAINAGE.

F ILL THE TERRARIUM WITH EVERYDAY THINGS YOU FIND IN NATURE: ROCKS, STICKS, WORMS AND INSECTS. IF YOU BUILD A REALLY LARGE ONE, YOU CAN TRY SMALL LIZARDS.

S MALL SHADE AND WATER-LOVING PLANTS ARE BEST, LIKE CLOVER OR SMALL FERNS. MOSSES AND LICHEN WORK VERY WELL, TOO!

B UT BEWARE! CREATURES NEED TO EAT! IF YOUR TERRARIUM CAN'T SUPPLY ENOUGH NUTRIENTS, YOU WILL HAVE TO FEED THEM.

P LACE THE JAR WHERE IT WILL RECEIVE PARTIAL SUNLIGHT. WATER ONCE IN THE BEGINNING, BUT NOT TOO MUCH, OR THE PLANTS WILL ROT. THE WATER VAPOR WILL STAY IN THE JAR AND BE CONTINUALLY RECYCLED.

Y OU CAN LEAVE THE TERRARIUM OPEN AT THE TOP BY PUTTING SMALL HOLES IN THE LID. THIS WAY IT CAN GET NUTRIENTS FROM THE OUTSIDE WORLD AND SURVIVE A LONG TIME. IF YOU SEAL IT COMPLETELY, YOU ARE RUNNING AN EXPERIMENT IN CLOSED ECOSYSTEMS. THE NUTRIENTS FROM THE SOIL FEED THE PLANTS, AND THE NUTRIENTS FROM THE PLANTS FEED THE INSECTS, AND THE CARBON DIOXIDE NEEDED BY ALL LIVING THINGS WILL HAVE TO BE BALANCED PERFECTLY BY THE WHOLE SYSTEM.

SELF-ASSEMBLY

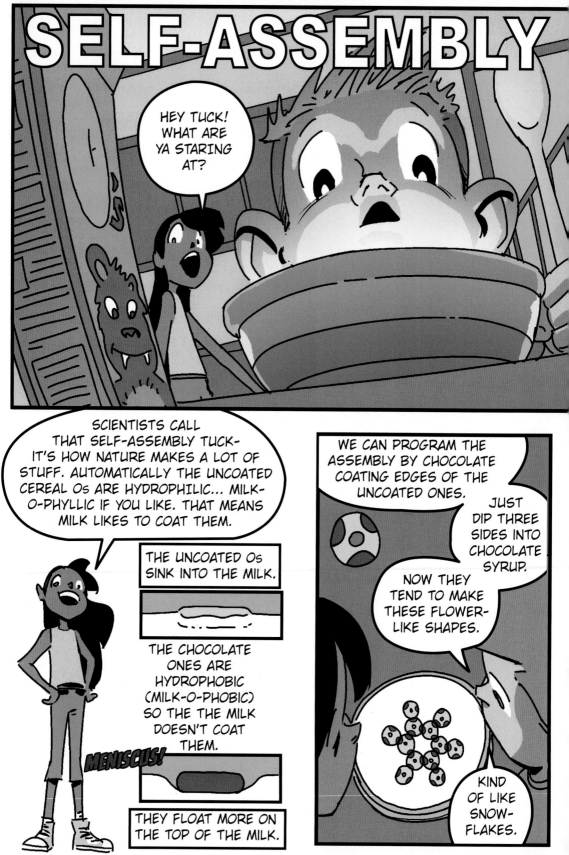

HEY TUCK! WHAT ARE YA STARING AT?

SCIENTISTS CALL THAT SELF-ASSEMBLY TUCK- IT'S HOW NATURE MAKES A LOT OF STUFF. AUTOMATICALLY THE UNCOATED CEREAL Os ARE HYDROPHILIC... MILK-O-PHYLLIC IF YOU LIKE. THAT MEANS MILK LIKES TO COAT THEM.

THE UNCOATED Os SINK INTO THE MILK.

THE CHOCOLATE ONES ARE HYDROPHOBIC (MILK-O-PHOBIC) SO THE THE MILK DOESN'T COAT THEM.

MENISCUS!

THEY FLOAT MORE ON THE TOP OF THE MILK.

WE CAN PROGRAM THE ASSEMBLY BY CHOCOLATE COATING EDGES OF THE UNCOATED ONES.

JUST DIP THREE SIDES INTO CHOCOLATE SYRUP.

NOW THEY TEND TO MAKE THESE FLOWER-LIKE SHAPES.

KIND OF LIKE SNOW-FLAKES.

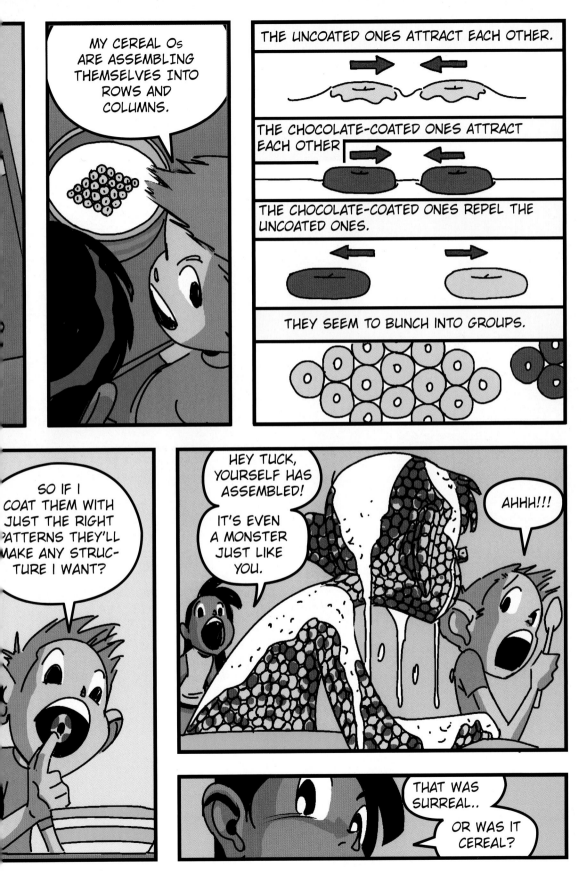

MY CEREAL Os ARE ASSEMBLING THEMSELVES INTO ROWS AND COLUMNS.

THE UNCOATED ONES ATTRACT EACH OTHER.

THE CHOCOLATE-COATED ONES ATTRACT EACH OTHER

THE CHOCOLATE-COATED ONES REPEL THE UNCOATED ONES.

THEY SEEM TO BUNCH INTO GROUPS.

SO IF I COAT THEM WITH JUST THE RIGHT PATTERNS THEY'LL MAKE ANY STRUCTURE I WANT?

HEY TUCK, YOURSELF HAS ASSEMBLED!

IT'S EVEN A MONSTER JUST LIKE YOU.

AHHH!!!

THAT WAS SURREAL..

OR WAS IT CEREAL?

"TO INVENT, YOU NEED A GOOD IMAGINATION AND A PILE OF JUNK."
– THOMAS A. EDISON

ENGINEERING

What is engineering? Is it science? Is it technology? Is it math? Is it art? Is it design or is it architecture? Engineering is all of these things. Sometimes engineering is the repair of complicated machinery with duct tape and chewing gum. Sometimes engineering involves strange tools and stranger techniques. In reality, engineering is just solving problems and enjoying it, designing machines and inventing systems. Engineers have built the world that is around us today, from the mundane to the high-flying. Sewer systems aren't glamorous but they save lives; rockets are fabulous, as are most things that fly. Toilets and toys, cars and candies, satellites and soccer balls, engineers have a hand in producing them all. Engineering is a vocation to be proud of, where you can produce things useful to yourself and others. The

great side effect of engineering is that it helps you have terrific hobbies, because engineering is the art of prototyping and perfecting, of building and making things. You'll never have to give up your Legos.

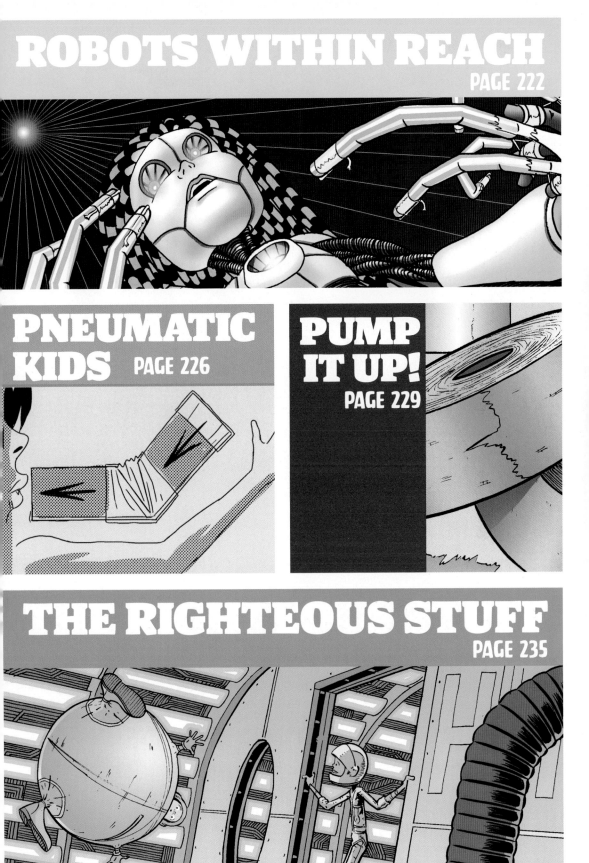

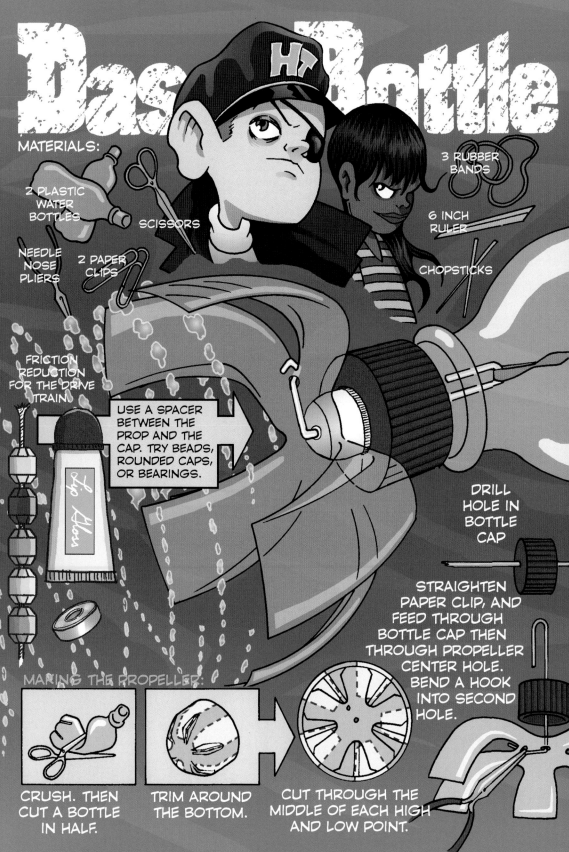

Das Bottle

MATERIALS:

2 PLASTIC WATER BOTTLES

SCISSORS

3 RUBBER BANDS

6 INCH RULER

CHOPSTICKS

NEEDLE NOSE PLIERS

2 PAPER CLIPS

FRICTION REDUCTION FOR THE DRIVE TRAIN

USE A SPACER BETWEEN THE PROP AND THE CAP. TRY BEADS, ROUNDED CAPS, OR BEARINGS.

DRILL HOLE IN BOTTLE CAP

STRAIGHTEN PAPER CLIP, AND FEED THROUGH BOTTLE CAP THEN THROUGH PROPELLER CENTER HOLE. BEND A HOOK INTO SECOND HOLE.

MAKING THE PROPELLER:

CRUSH. THEN CUT A BOTTLE IN HALF.

TRIM AROUND THE BOTTOM.

CUT THROUGH THE MIDDLE OF EACH HIGH AND LOW POINT.

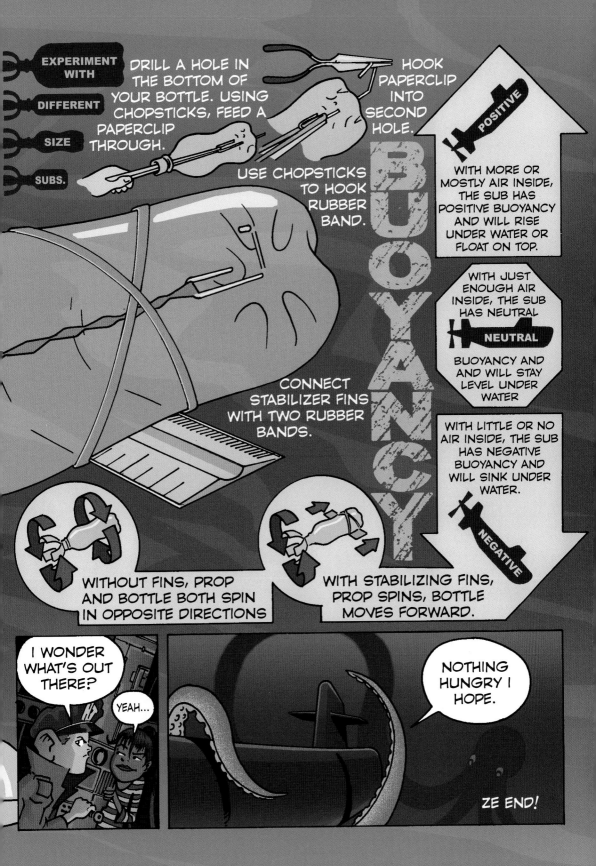

SPRING-LOADED CHOPSTICKS

DŌMO ARIGATŌ TUCKER SAN.

USE CHOPSTICKS AND CLOTHES PIN.   REPLACE WOOD OF CLOTHES PIN WITH CHOPSTICK.

BAKA

MO

ICHI -

GEI.

SPRING-LOADED CHOPSTICKS HAVE MANY USES SUCH AS EATING UTENSILS AND TWEEZERS.

NICK DRAGOTTA - JOOST BONSEN - SAUL GRIFFITH

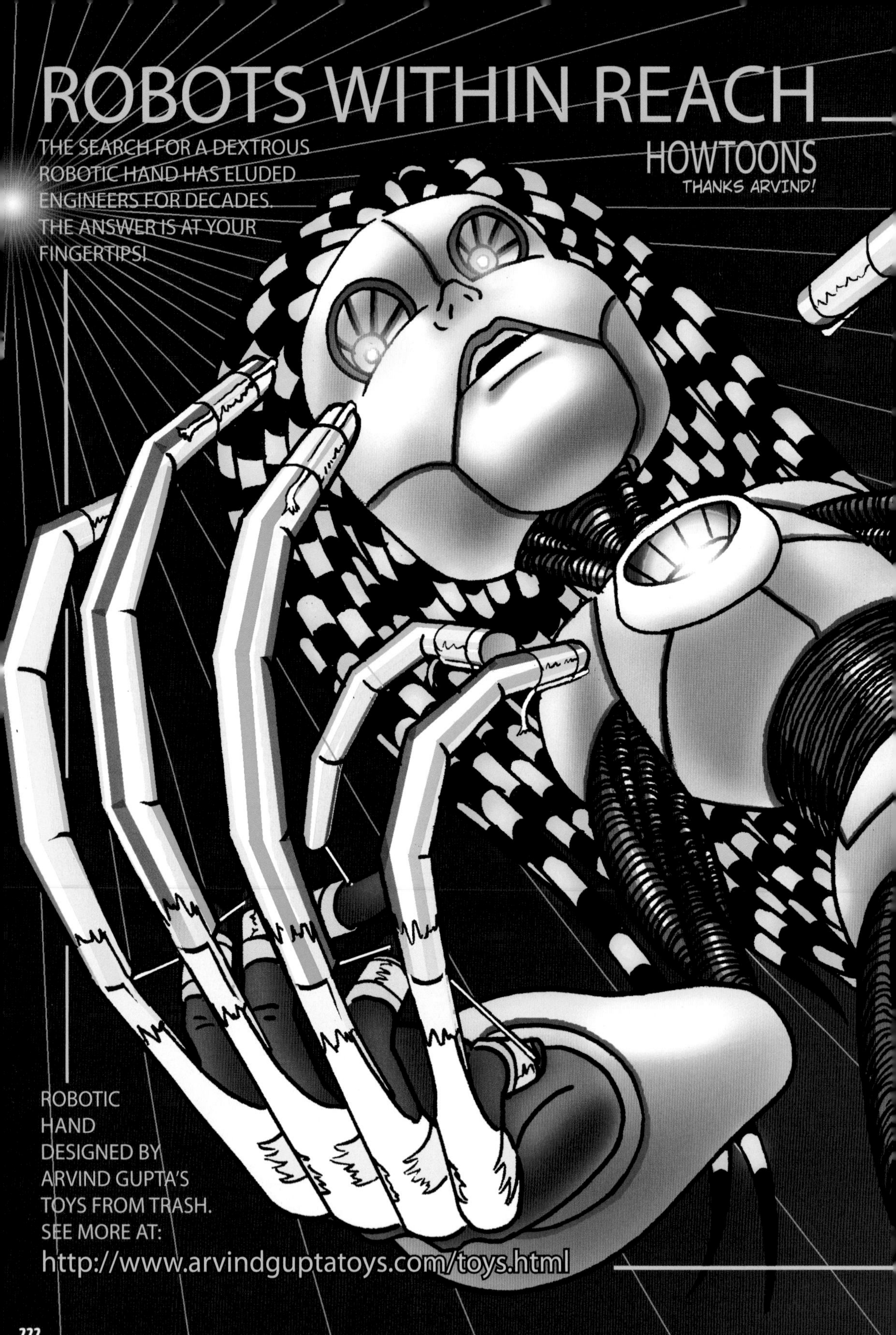

ROBOTS WITHIN REACH__

THE SEARCH FOR A DEXTROUS
ROBOTIC HAND HAS ELUDED
ENGINEERS FOR DECADES.
THE ANSWER IS AT YOUR
FINGERTIPS!

HOWTOONS
THANKS ARVIND!

ROBOTIC
HAND
DESIGNED BY
ARVIND GUPTA'S
TOYS FROM TRASH.
SEE MORE AT:
http://www.arvindguptatoys.com/toys.html

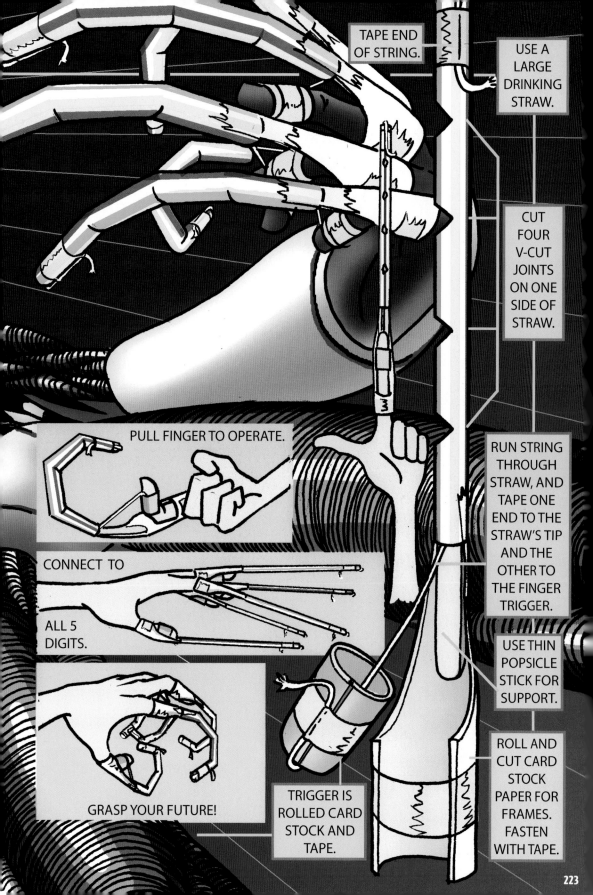

TAPE END OF STRING.

USE A LARGE DRINKING STRAW.

CUT FOUR V-CUT JOINTS ON ONE SIDE OF STRAW.

PULL FINGER TO OPERATE.

CONNECT TO ALL 5 DIGITS.

RUN STRING THROUGH STRAW, AND TAPE ONE END TO THE STRAW'S TIP AND THE OTHER TO THE FINGER TRIGGER.

USE THIN POPSICLE STICK FOR SUPPORT.

GRASP YOUR FUTURE!

TRIGGER IS ROLLED CARD STOCK AND TAPE.

ROLL AND CUT CARD STOCK PAPER FOR FRAMES. FASTEN WITH TAPE.

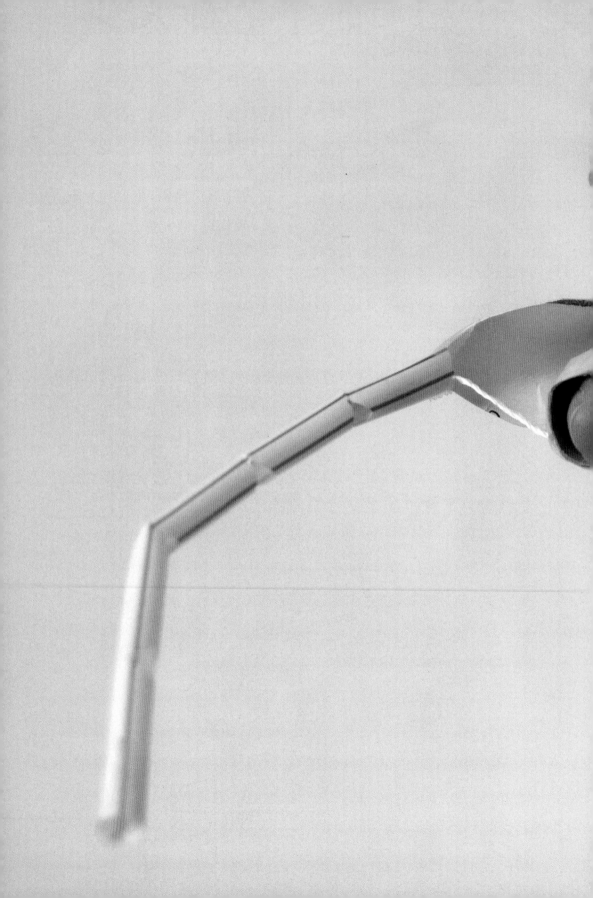

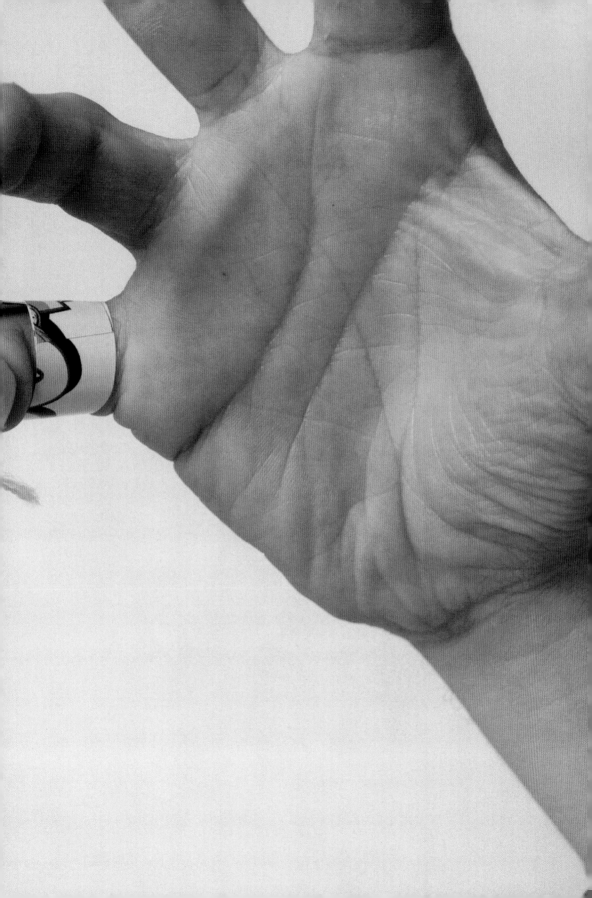

THE PNEUMATIC KIDS
WOW!
WE WOULDN'T NEED TECHNOLOGY IF SUPERPOWERS WERE REALLY POSSIBLE!
TO GAIN EXTRA STRENGTH, WE NEED MORE MUSCLES, OR "ACTUATORS" AS TECHIES CALL THEM.
TO POWER OUR MUSCLES, WE CAN DEVELOP NEW PNEUMATIC TECHNOLOGIES OR AIR-POWERED MUSCLES.
WE CAN MAKE THESE PNEUMATIC MUSCLES BY USING PRESSURIZED AIR CANISTERS CONNECTED TO A NETWORK OF HOSES THAT ADD AND SUBTRACT AIR, MOVING THE 23 DIFFERENT MUSCLES OF THE ARM.

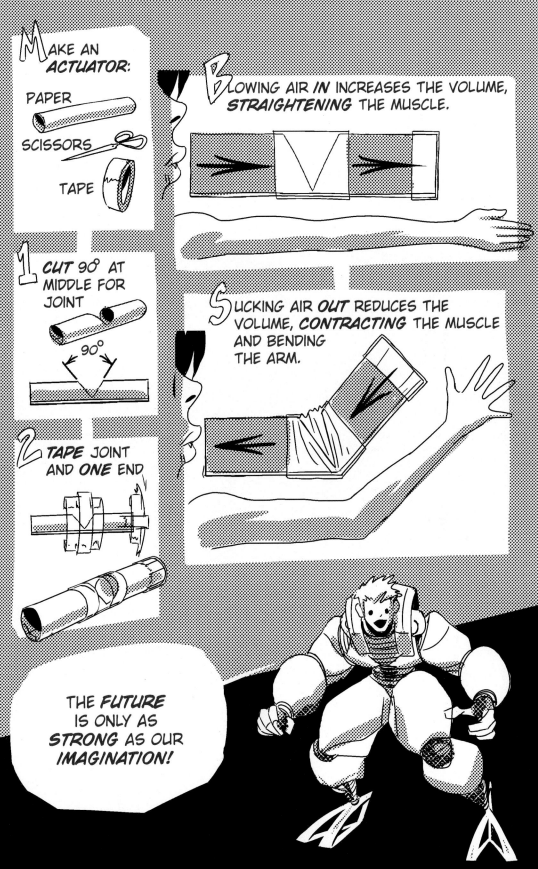

MAKE AN **ACTUATOR:**

PAPER

SCISSORS

TAPE

1 **CUT** 90° AT MIDDLE FOR JOINT

90°

2 **TAPE** JOINT AND **ONE** END

BLOWING AIR **IN** INCREASES THE VOLUME, **STRAIGHTENING** THE MUSCLE.

SUCKING AIR **OUT** REDUCES THE VOLUME, **CONTRACTING** THE MUSCLE AND BENDING THE ARM.

THE **FUTURE** IS ONLY AS **STRONG** AS OUR **IMAGINATION!**

EVEN GROWNUPS NEED TO MAKE PROTOTYPES AND TEST THEIR IDEAS! THIS IS AN EARLY MODEL OF AN EXOSKELETON PROJECT BEING MADE BY OTHERLAB IN SAN FRANCISCO. JUST LIKE THE PROJECT HERE, IT USES TUBES OF AIR TO POWER EXTERNAL "MUSCLES."

234

THE RIGHTEOUS STUFF

GO WHERE NO KID HAS GONE BEFORE

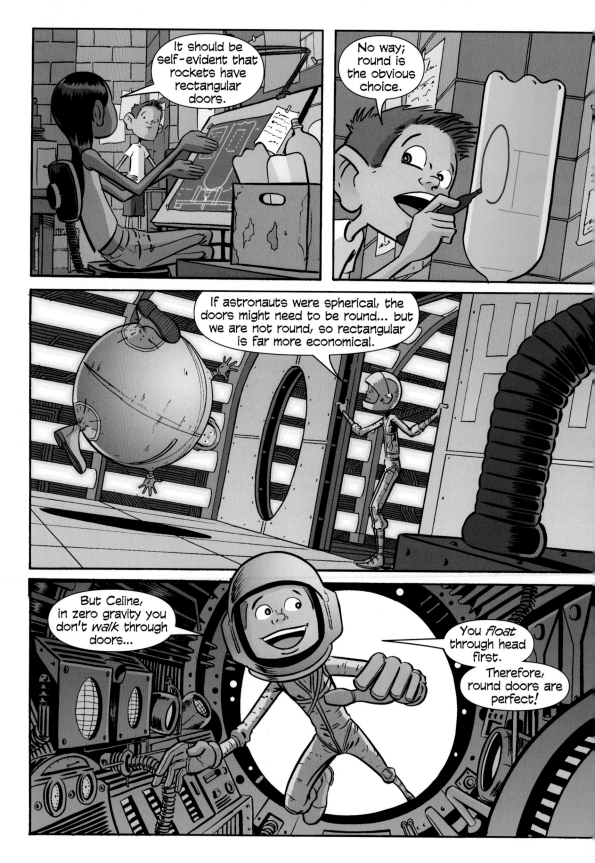

237

I'll launch first.

Fine! Let's set 'em up.

Ready, Tuck?

My systems are go.

Me too!

238

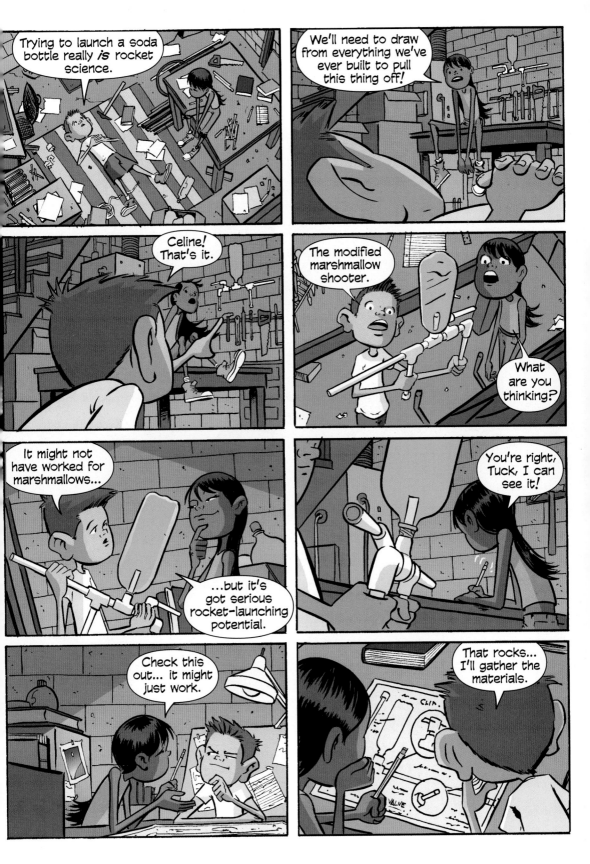

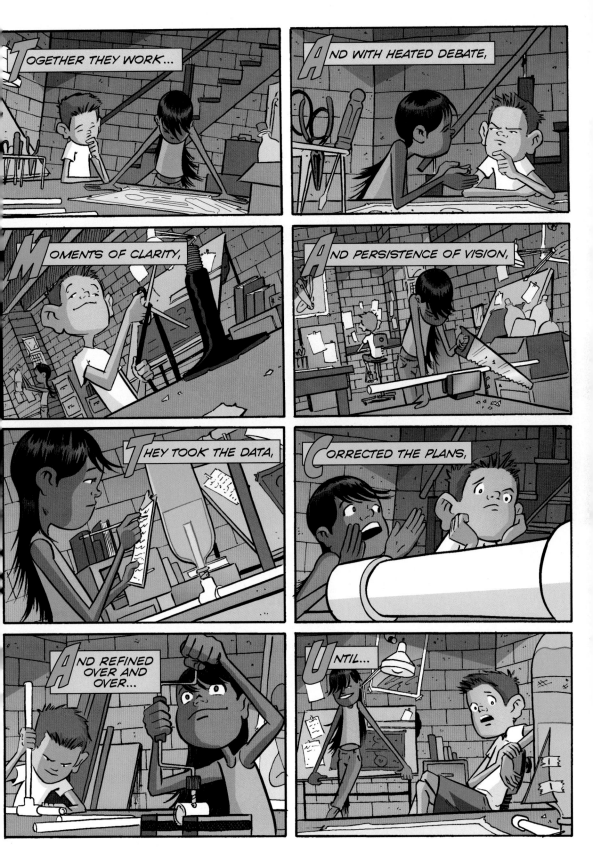

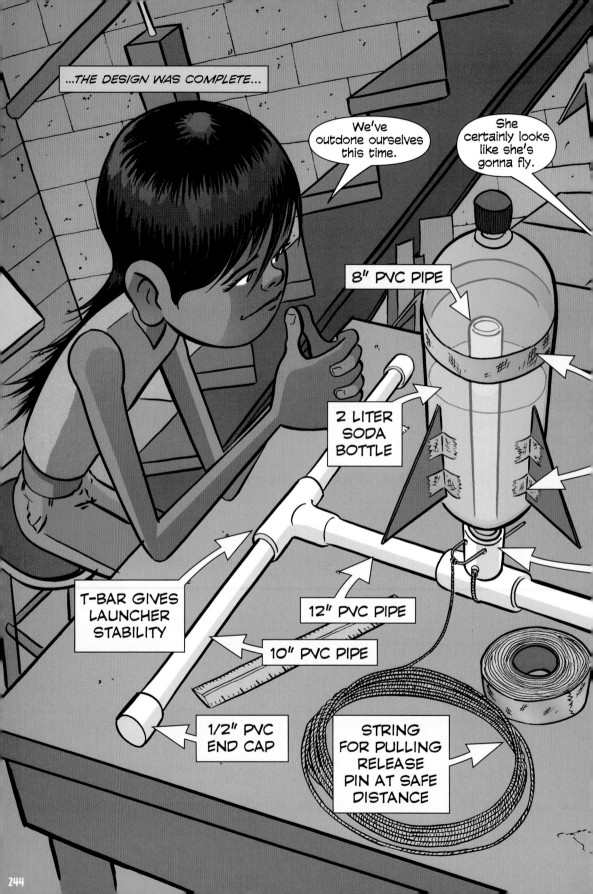

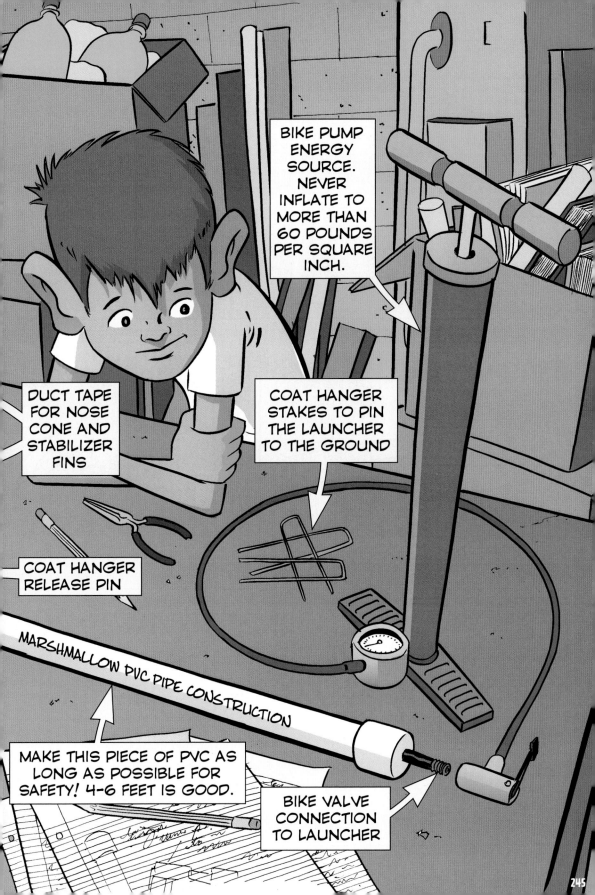

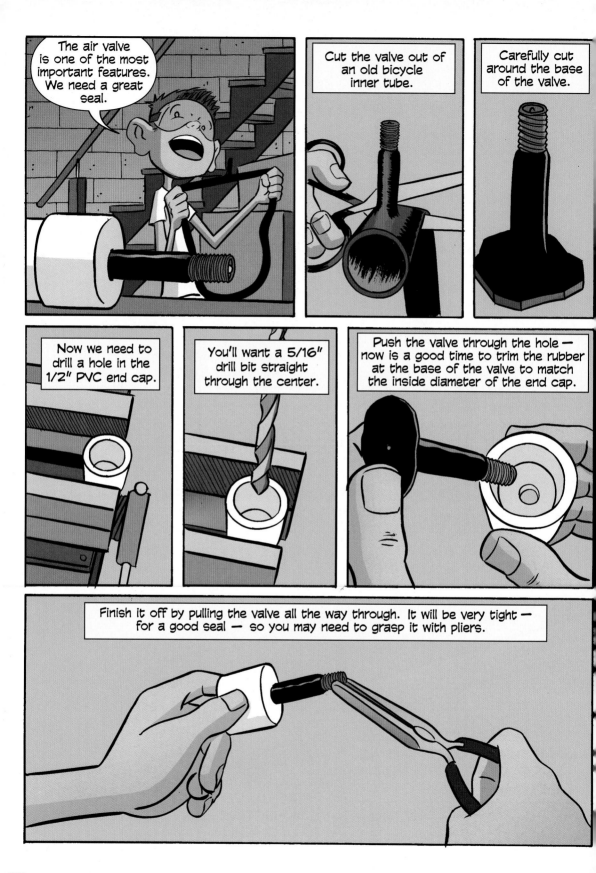

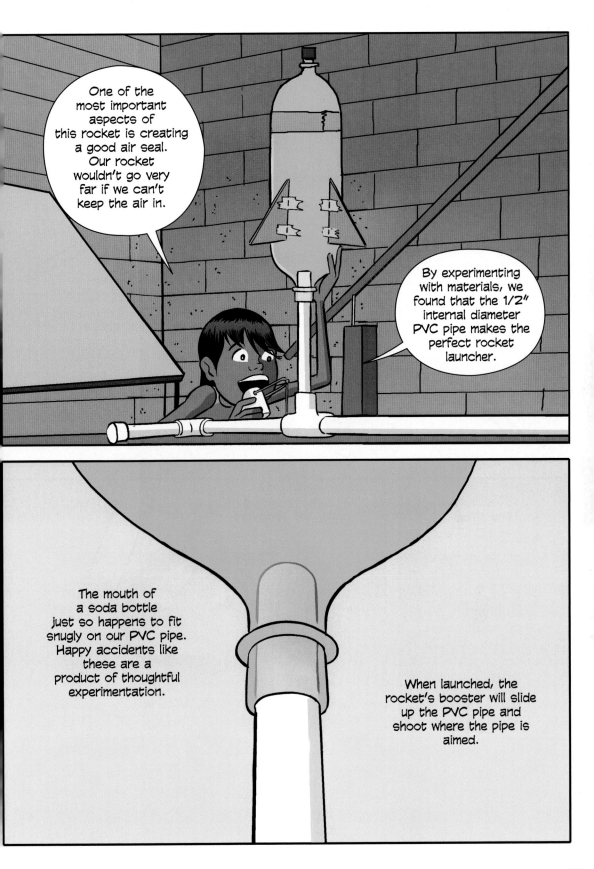

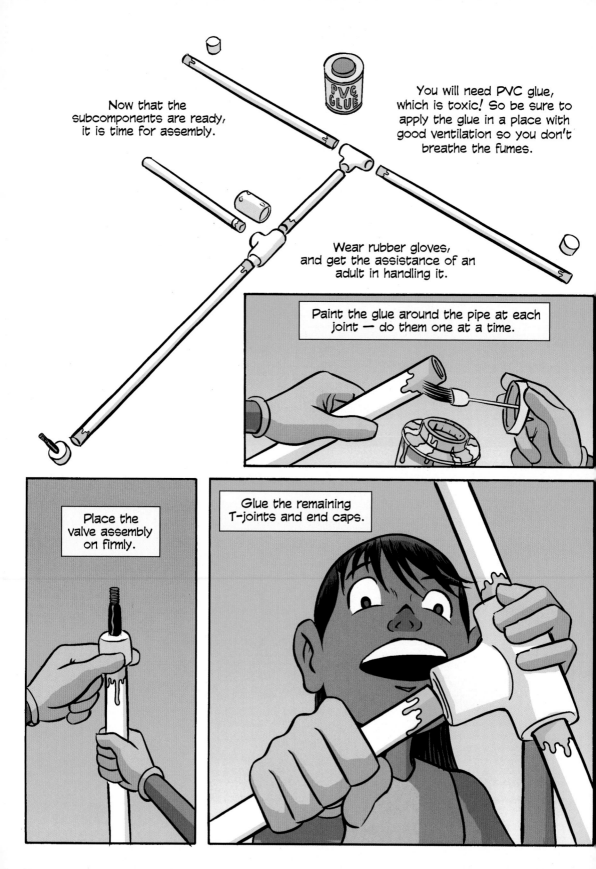

Now that the subcomponents are ready, it is time for assembly.

You will need PVC glue, which is toxic! So be sure to apply the glue in a place with good ventilation so you don't breathe the fumes.

Wear rubber gloves, and get the assistance of an adult in handling it.

Paint the glue around the pipe at each joint — do them one at a time.

Place the valve assembly on firmly.

Glue the remaining T-joints and end caps.

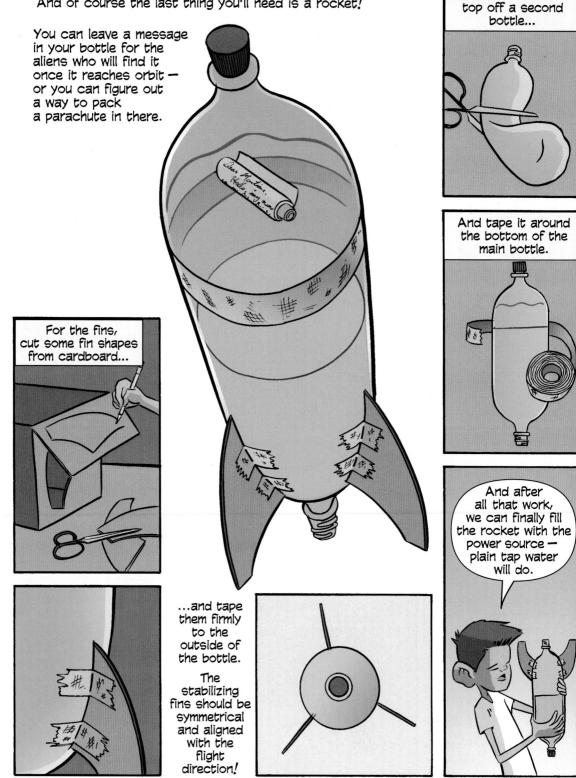

And of course the last thing you'll need is a rocket!

You can leave a message in your bottle for the aliens who will find it once it reaches orbit — or you can figure out a way to pack a parachute in there.

For the aerodynamic nose cone, cut the top off a second bottle...

And tape it around the bottom of the main bottle.

For the fins, cut some fin shapes from cardboard...

...and tape them firmly to the outside of the bottle.

The stabilizing fins should be symmetrical and aligned with the flight direction!

And after all that work, we can finally fill the rocket with the power source — plain tap water will do.

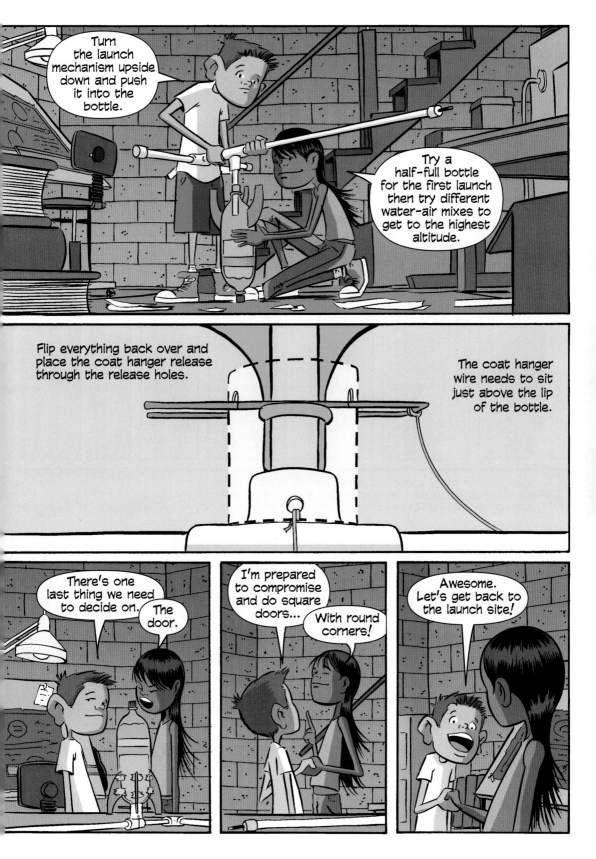

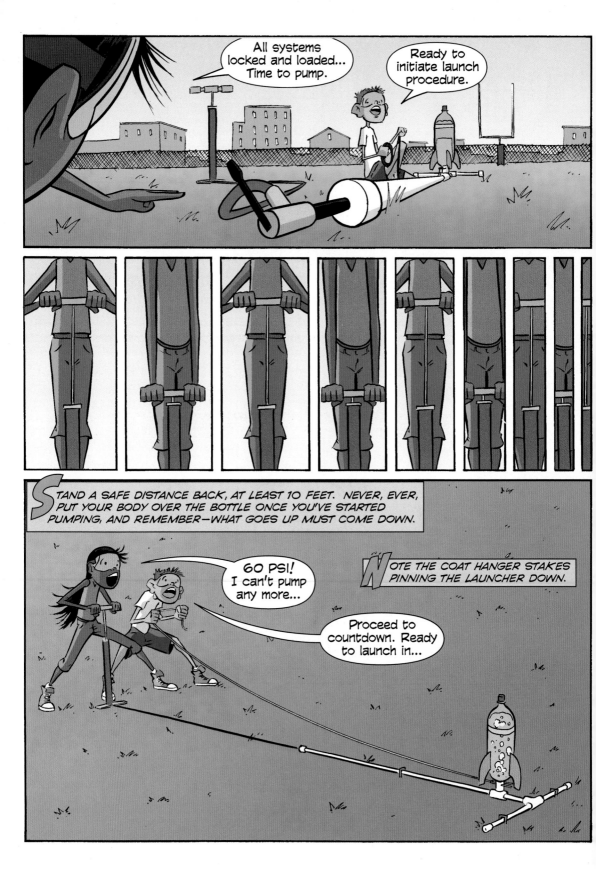

PiNG

"TRY AGAIN.
FAIL AGAIN.
FAIL BETTER."
– SAMUEL BECKETT

DESIGN & PROCESS

What is design? Why is it different to art, or craft, or science or music or writing… Stepping back we might broadly call all of these things human creativity. They all overlap. When working best they play and dance with each other, they embrace and talk and produce things together that any one of the individuals cannot produce alone. If you are engaging in any one of these activities it is healthy to understand that you are really engaging them all, and the more of them you engage, the greater and richer your adventures as a human being can be. But design takes whatever thing that you made, and refines it. It makes sure that your invention is as streamlined and elegant as can be. Good design makes good ideas even better.

Wouldn't it be wonderful if all youth were curious learners like Tucker and Celine?

Tucker and Celine are budding scientists and inventors. They're confident in their abilities to acquire knowledge and develop new skills – no problem is too big for them to tackle. Whether they are doodling while contemplating cave wall paintings or selecting the right tool for the job, Tucker and Celine are curious and have fun finding good problems in need of solutions.

As the invention education officer for the Lemelson-MIT Program, I've had the pleasure of collaborating with the wonderful folks who created Tucker and Celine as an amalgam of what's possible when youth are thoroughly engaged with their own learning. Saul, Joost, Nick, Ingrid, Ryan, Jeff, and Sandy have all added their own love of hands-on learning through their storytelling and illustrating. They inspire youth to create their own workshop for "mass construction" and to fill buckets with tools and duct tape so they're always ready to repair, create, and invent. Oh, what I wouldn't give to have an organized workshop like Tucker and Celine's!

Seeing the Future! A Guide to Visual Communication (2010) was developed out of my experience working with young inventors in high school who couldn't easily share their ideas with each other. Words were insufficient to describe what they "saw" in their mind. They were intimidated to draw which hindered collaboration and progress. Art often becomes an elective subject in high school enjoyed by only a few. Do you remember how fun it was to draw in elementary school? I do. Unfortunately, many of us leave this fun behind as we grow up. Tucker and Celine help us find that fun in drawing again so we can share our good ideas.

Playground (2014) was created because I found many young inventors had ideas for technological solutions but lacked the tools to build basic prototypes. Youth need to understand the importance of selecting the right tool for the job and to develop good habits for using tools safely. Young inventors can borrow or affordably purchase appropriate tools for building prototypes if they are resourceful. Tucker and Celine are experts at being resourceful – a key trait of inventors – and find tools in their community. They share their knowledge of drills, hammers, and saws in an informative, fun way while building a playground.

Seeing the Future! and Playground focus on the design of solutions and the process of inventing. Technological solutions can be developed in an experiential manner through iterative trial and error. Young inventors often work through the inventing process this way. The Lemelson-MIT Program doesn't provide a step-by-step process for inventing, but we do insist that designing a solution starts with being empathetic to the needs of others. Inventors must work with a beneficiary of the solution. In Playground, Tucker and Celine's beneficiary is their neighborhood that doesn't have a safe area for youth to play. Having and working with a beneficiary helps ensure that the solution will be useful.

Designing and building solutions require teamwork. Good, collaborative teamwork builds upon the knowledge and skills of each member. Individually, neither Tucker nor Celine would be able to accomplish what they do together. This is the real world. Inventing resembles a team sport and relies on the minds-on knowledge and hands-on skills of all members. Tinkerers, doodlers, communicators, and organizers are all necessary to make an invention real.

Young inventors rely on the expertise and guidance of adults. Tucker and Celine rely on Mr. Hama in Playground. Young inventors associated with the Lemelson-MIT Program rely on educators, makers, inventors, engineers, tradesmen, and professionals who have

knowledge and skills that they have yet to develop. Call them mentors – or simply caring adults – these are people who help guide young inventors through the knowledge and skill acquisition experiences necessary for them to build their useful idea that will help others.

As a parent and an educator, I've experienced how easy it can be to motivate and engage youth in their own learning outside of the school day through minds-on and hands-on learning. This is where youth have time to experiment, be creative, and learn from their failures. Parents and educators need to encourage youth to be active in their learning, nurture their curiosity, and encourage them to be empathic to the needs of others. Always ask, "Have you found a good problem to solve?" Youth will have fun learning while building the confidence they need to be the inventors of tomorrow with a good problem, a beneficiary, tools, teammates, mentors, and the green light to fail.

-Leigh B. Estabrooks

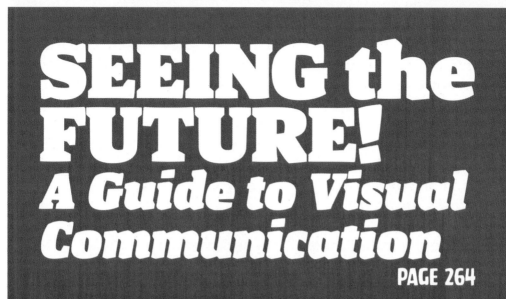

SEEING the FUTURE!
A Guide to Visual Communication
PAGE 264

LET'S BUILD A PLAY-GROUND!

PAGE 304

DRAW TUCKER & CELINE

PAGE 330

SOLID
SHAPE

SEEING the FUTURE!
A Guide to Visual Communication

presented by

HOWTOONS and the

Tuck... *You* might not realize it yet, but *everyone* can draw!

Since the *dawn* of man we have used *pictures, drawings, symbols,* and *doodles* to share *ideas* to *communicate*.

In *500 BC* the *Greeks* shared their *ideas through art.* From murals on the walls to potraits on wood, the Greeks *shared* their *history* and recorded their *culture*.

In the **Stone Age**, cavemen painted nearly **2,000** images on a cave wall in Lascaux, France. These paintings depicted *humans, animals,* and *symbols*... *What* were they *trying* to *tell* us?

Inspired by the Greeks, the Italian **Renaissance** saw great progress in the visual arts. *New technologies* gave people the tools to **communicate** advancing *ideas.*

Nobody defined **Renaissance Man** better than *Leonardo da Vinci.* Inventor, artist, engineer, architect, and scientist, he did it all.

Although we cherish his fine art, it is through his *notebooks* that we get inspired by his *genius.* He shows a *future, imagined* before its time: flying machines, solar and hydrodynamic energy, ideas on optics, weaponry, studies of botany and anatomy.

Since the Renaissance the *intersection* of art, science, and invention has continued to merge and propel us forward.

Whether it be *artists, engineers, scientists, inventors,* or *designers,* all great *achievements* start with a humble *doodle.*

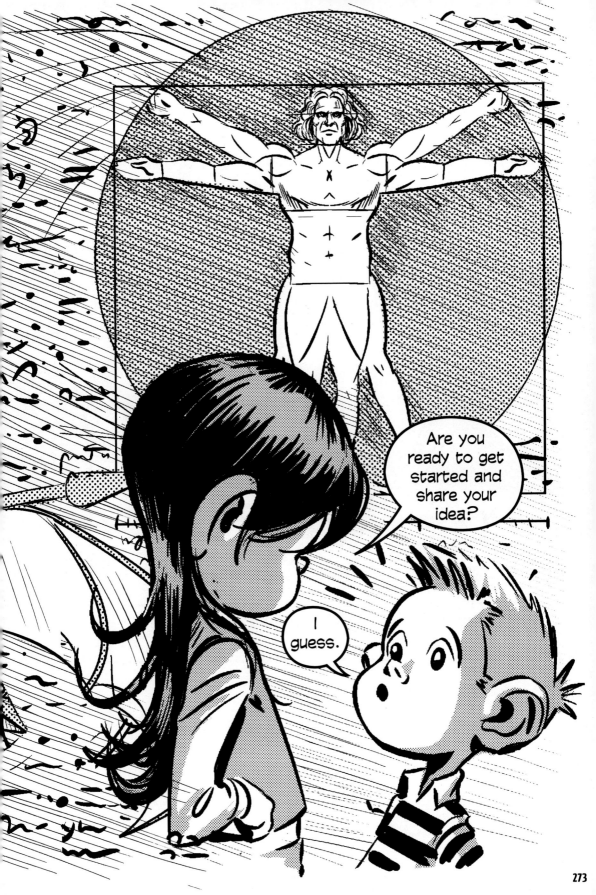

These lines can work together in a variety of ways. By training your artist's eye we can draw them to communicate, like the shapes below.

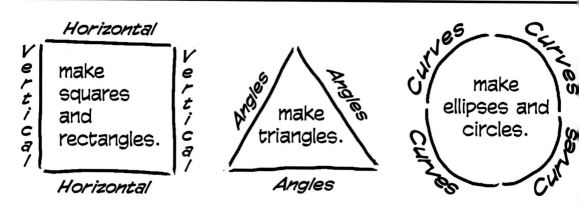

Horizontal
Vertical / Vertical

make squares and rectangles.

Horizontal

Angles / Angles

make triangles.

Angles

Curves / Curves

make ellipses and circles.

Curves / Curves

...draw horizontal lines? Keep'em straight and parallel to the ground plane.

Draw vertical lines. Straight up and down.

Try angled lines.

Now curves, like rainbows!

It's *all* about *learning* the basics.

It's easy to draw once you learn to break down the shapes.

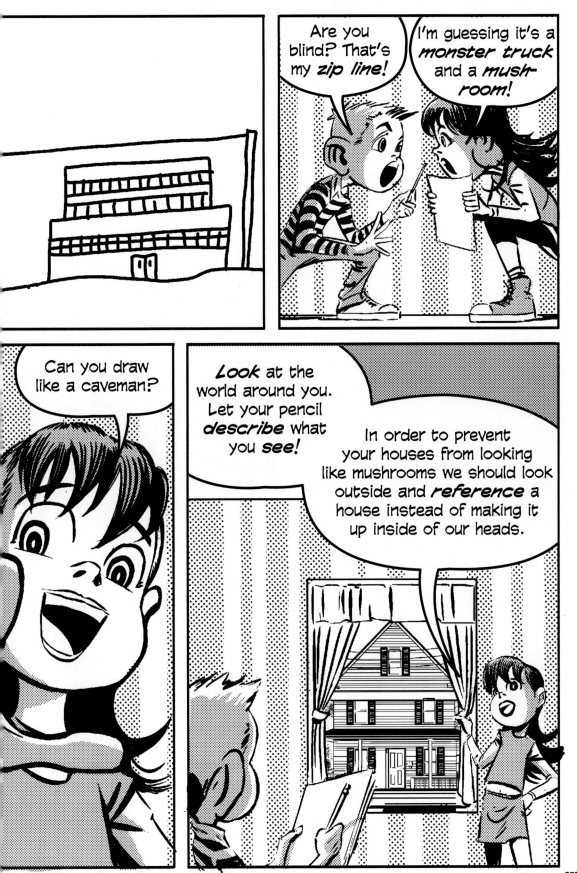

We can improve our drawing by looking at how lines and shape relate to one another! It's called *proportion*.

See the spatial relationships and record it on paper.

Always ask yourself questions when you draw.

Is the house taller than it is wide?

Where does the tree line fall on the house?

Why make it up if you don't have to.

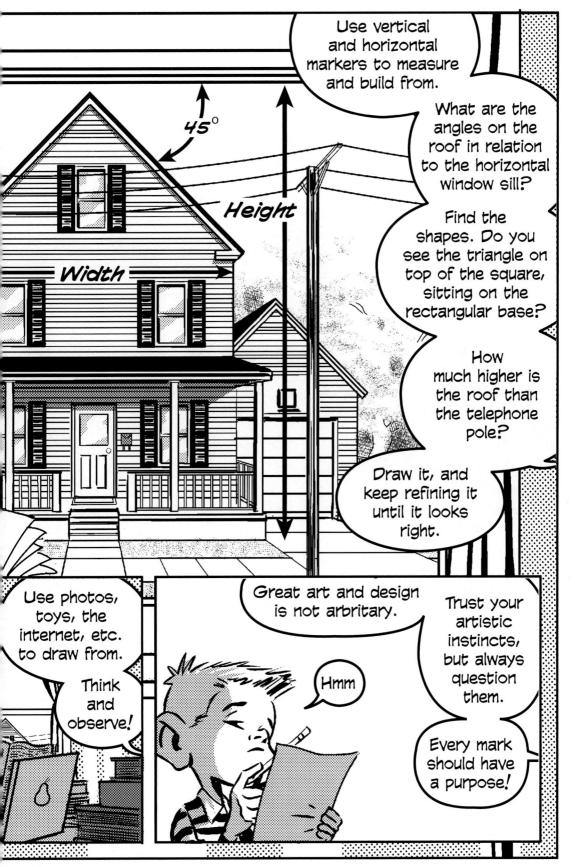

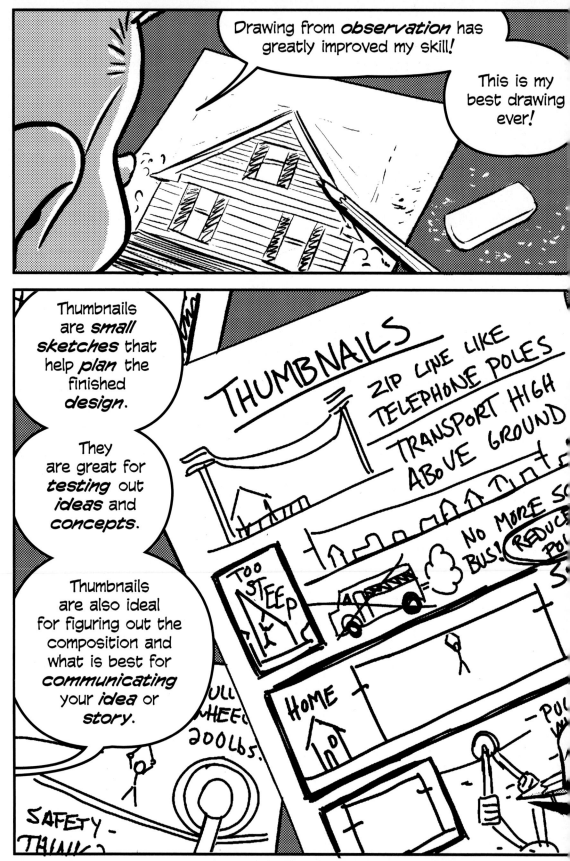

Drawing from *observation* has greatly improved my skill!

This is my best drawing ever!

Thumbnails are *small sketches* that help *plan* the finished *design*.

They are great for *testing* out *ideas* and *concepts*.

Thumbnails are also ideal for figuring out the composition and what is best for *communicating* your *idea* or *story*.

THUMBNAILS

ZIP LINE LIKE TELEPHONE POLES

TRANSPORT HIGH ABOVE GROUND

NO MORE S BUS! REDUCE POL

TOO STEEP

HOME

ULL WHEE 200Lbs.

SAFETY - THINK

"*Depth* is crucial in *creating* the *illusion* of believable *space* on paper."

"And artists use *perspective* to draw that *believable space*."

"Hold your *thumbs* up at eye level. From my viewpoint your thumbs ar the same size. There is *no depth!* Your thumbs are *parallel* to the picture plane. We can illustrate that by drawing parallel lines above an below your hands."

HORIZON LINE

NO DEPTH

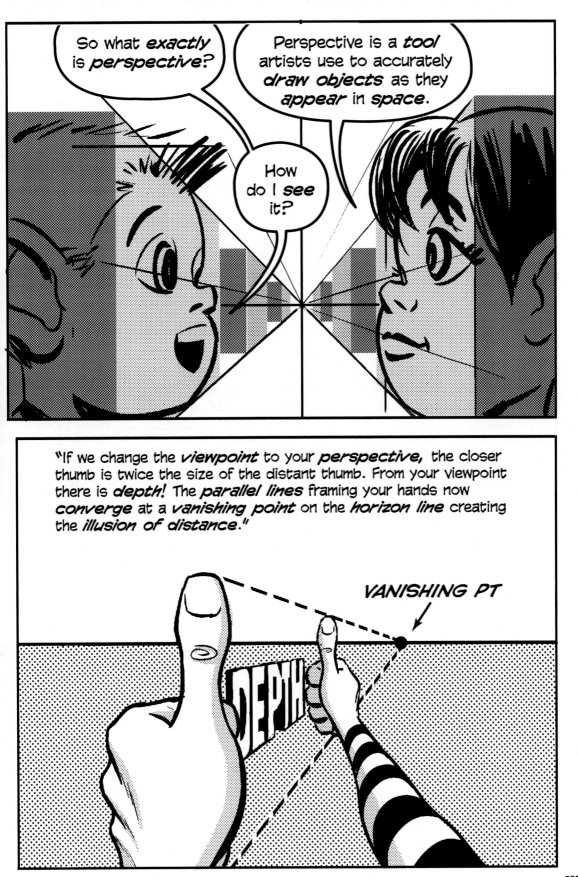

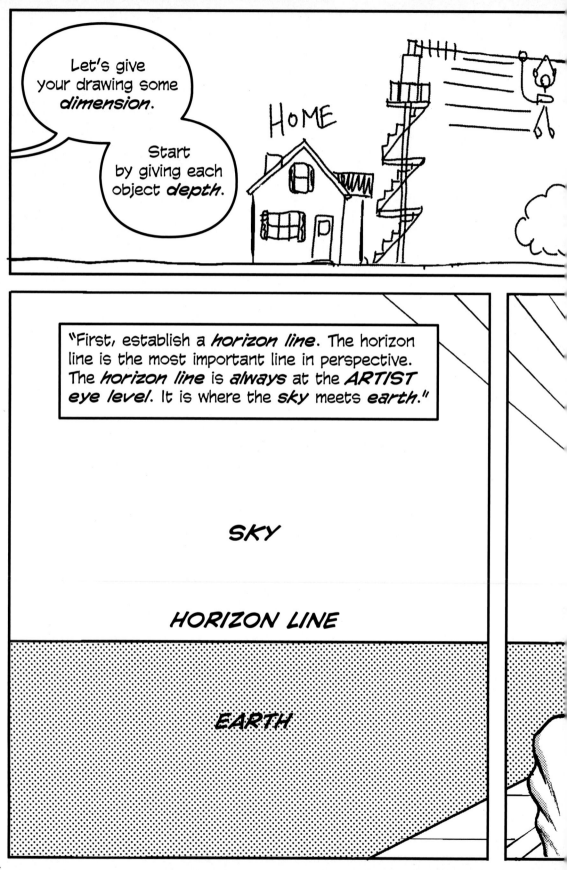

Let's give your drawing some *dimension*.

Start by giving each object *depth*.

HOME

"First, establish a *horizon line*. The horizon line is the most important line in perspective. The *horizon line* is *always* at the *ARTIST eye level*. It is where the *sky* meets *earth*."

SKY

HORIZON LINE

EARTH

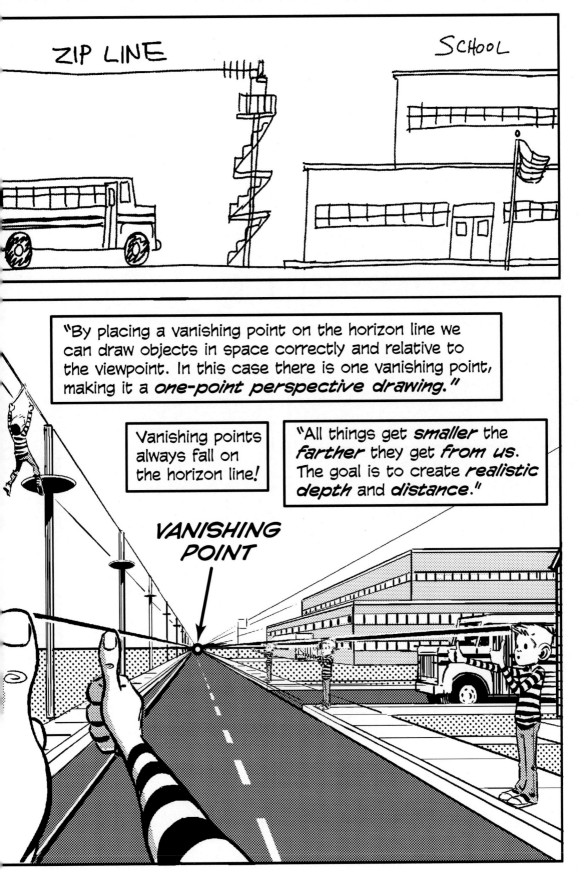

ZIP LINE

SCHOOL

"By placing a vanishing point on the horizon line we can draw objects in space correctly and relative to the viewpoint. In this case there is one vanishing point, making it a *one-point perspective drawing.*"

Vanishing points always fall on the horizon line!

"All things get *smaller* the *farther* they get *from us.* The goal is to create *realistic depth* and *distance.*"

VANISHING POINT

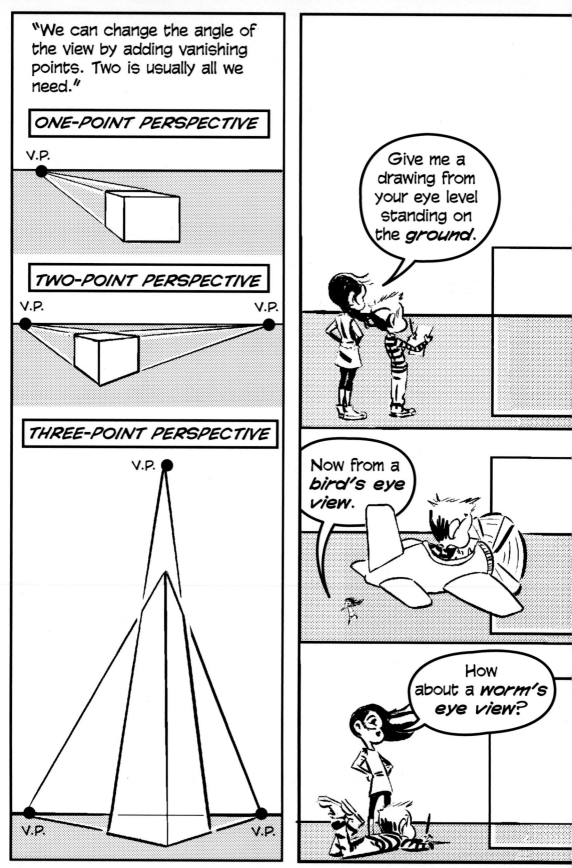

Look at how dramatic the effect is when we move the horizon line (the artist's view point). Like a movie director, you choose the shot that is best for your drawing.

Like art, video games also progressed from flat...

to games with one-point perspective...

to games with two-point perspective...

to fully immersive 3-D worlds.

Now that we have a basic understanding of perspective, we need to keep those principles in mind when drawing.

"All objects can be broken down into simple geometric shapes: spheres, cubes, cones, cylinders, or a combination there of. If you remember this rule and keep in mind how they relate to the horizon line (perspective) you will be able to draw anything."

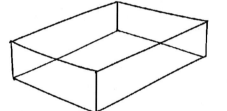

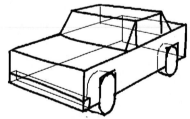

It is not necessary to draw perspective grids for everything. With enough practice we can imagine the lines going back into space and meeting at a vanishing point. Try boxing it up!

Imagine a box projecting back in space. If our line strays outside of the box the house will look wrong. Create the illusion of parallel lines going back in space.

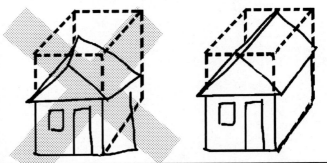

The most important thing an artist can do is *practice*. The more you draw with *careful observation* and attention to these principles the better your drawings will be.

Thanks Celine! With practice, this will really bring my invention to life.

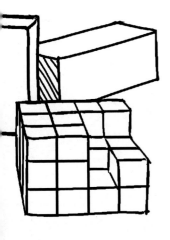

PRESENTED BY **HOWTOONS** AND *THE LEMELSON-MIT INVENTEAMS.*

WRITTEN BY JEFF PARKER, ART BY SANDY JARREL, EDITS BY LEIGH ESTABROOKS

305

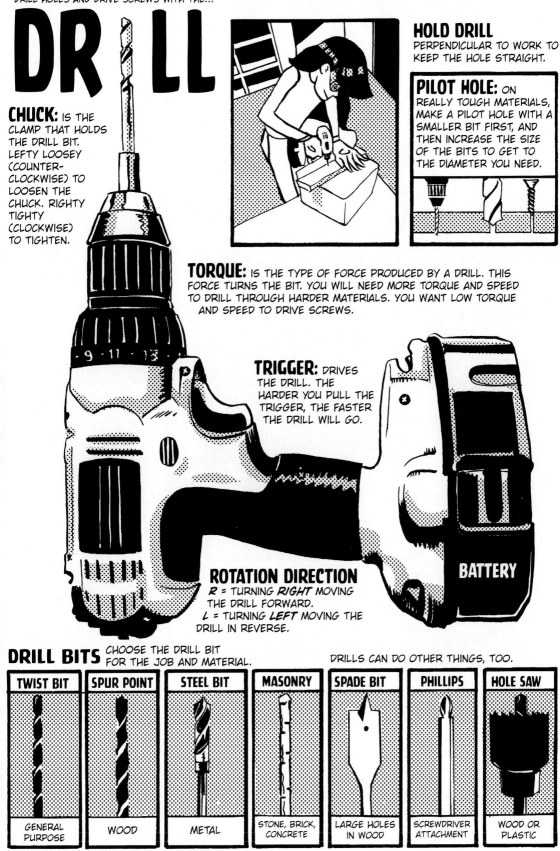

DRILL HOLES AND DRIVE SCREWS WITH THE...

DR LL

CHUCK: IS THE CLAMP THAT HOLDS THE DRILL BIT. LEFTY LOOSEY (COUNTER-CLOCKWISE) TO LOOSEN THE CHUCK. RIGHTY TIGHTY (CLOCKWISE) TO TIGHTEN.

HOLD DRILL
PERPENDICULAR TO WORK TO KEEP THE HOLE STRAIGHT.

PILOT HOLE: ON REALLY TOUGH MATERIALS, MAKE A PILOT HOLE WITH A SMALLER BIT FIRST, AND THEN INCREASE THE SIZE OF THE BITS TO GET TO THE DIAMETER YOU NEED.

TORQUE: IS THE TYPE OF FORCE PRODUCED BY A DRILL. THIS FORCE TURNS THE BIT. YOU WILL NEED MORE TORQUE AND SPEED TO DRILL THROUGH HARDER MATERIALS. YOU WANT LOW TORQUE AND SPEED TO DRIVE SCREWS.

TRIGGER: DRIVES THE DRILL. THE HARDER YOU PULL THE TRIGGER, THE FASTER THE DRILL WILL GO.

9 · 11 · 13

BATTERY

ROTATION DIRECTION
R = TURNING **RIGHT** MOVING THE DRILL FORWARD.
L = TURNING **LEFT** MOVING THE DRILL IN REVERSE.

DRILL BITS
CHOOSE THE DRILL BIT FOR THE JOB AND MATERIAL.

DRILLS CAN DO OTHER THINGS, TOO.

TWIST BIT	SPUR POINT	STEEL BIT	MASONRY	SPADE BIT	PHILLIPS	HOLE SAW
GENERAL PURPOSE	WOOD	METAL	STONE, BRICK, CONCRETE	LARGE HOLES IN WOOD	SCREWDRIVER ATTACHMENT	WOOD OR PLASTIC

GET STARTED
TIME TO GET TO WORK! PICK THE SIMPLEST PROJECT FIRST SO YOU CAN SEE RESULTS FASTER, AND BUILD YOUR SKILLS AS YOU GO.

THIS TREE LOOKS HEALTHY AND HAS STRONG BRANCHES. IT WOULD BE GREAT FOR A SWING!

MATERIALS AND TOOLS:
-CIRCLE OF WOOD 1 1/2" X 12"
-50 FEET OF ROPE AT LEAST 1/4" THICK
-DRILL
-CLAMPS

FIND A GOOD SOLID WOOD SEAT- LIKE SAY THE TOP OF AN OLD KITCHEN STOOL! CLAMP THE WOOD SEAT TO SECURELY HOLD IT. DRILL A HOLE IN THE CENTER.

TO FIND THE LENGTH OF THE ROPE, MEASURE THE DISTANCE OF THE BRANCH TO THE GROUND AND DOUBLE THE AMOUNT OF ROPE.

FIND A DRILL BIT THE SAME DIAMETER TO MATCH THE THICKNESS OF THE ROPE. USE A SPADE BIT OR A HOLE SAW.

YOU MAY WANT TO START A PILOT HOLE WITH A SMALLER BIT TO MAKE IT GO EASIER.

LET'S BUILD A **ZIP LINE!**

THIS LOOKS LIKE A GREAT SPOT TO PUT OUR ZIPLINE. NOT TOO MUCH INCLINE AND THE LAND IS FLAT AND FREE OF DEBRIS!

MATERIALS:
ZIPLINE:
-1/4" GALVANIZED WIRE CABLE (MEASURE BETWEEN TREES FOR LENGTH)
-1 1/4" ALUMINUM WIRE SWAGE
-3 1/4" CABLE CLAMPS
-2 RATCHET STRAPS
-2 QUICK LINK
-LADDER
HANDLE:
-2 WHEEL PULLEY
-STEEL CARABINER
-HANDLE BARS
SAFETY:
-4"X4"X6" WOODEN BLOCK
-20 FT BUNGEE CORD
-6" EYELET BOLT
-SAND OR MULCH

RATCHET STRAP

QUICK LINK

1/4" WIRE WITH ALUMINUM WIRE SWAGE

LOOP WIRE THROUGH SWAGE AND HAMMER TO FLATTEN SHUT.

THREAD WEBBING THROUGH RATCHET

OPEN AND CLOSE THE RATCHET TO TIGHTEN THE STRAP

OPEN

CLOSE

REPURPOSED BIKE HANDLE-BARS

PLANT STAKE FOR GROUND ANCHOR SO BUNGEE STRETCHES TO SLOWLY STOP THE PULLEY

TREES ARE A GOOD SUPPORT FOR THE ZIPLINE BECAUSE THE WEIGHT GETS DISTRIBUTED THROUGH THE ROOTS MAKING THE ANCHORS STURDY AND SECURE.

FOR A SAFE SPEED, MAKE THE DECLINE 3 FEET FOR EVERY 50 FEET OF LENGTH.

USE 3 CABLE CLAMPS SPACED 3" APART TO CREATE A LOOP AND DOUBLE THE CABLE BACK ON ITSELF. THE BOLTS SHOULD ALL FACE THE LIVE END OF THE CABLE.

LIVE (LONG) END

DEAD (SHORT) END

WOOD STOPPING BLOCK

BUNGEE CORD

DRILL A 5/16" HOLE IN TOP OF THE BLOCK

DRILL A 1/4" HOLE TO THE SIDE OF THE BLOCK

INSERT EYELET BOLT INTO THE SIDE HOLE

THREAD CABLE WIRE THROUGH THE BLOCK

TIE BUNGEE TO BOLT USING A FIGURE-8 KNOT

TIE BUNGEE TO STAKE USING A FIGURE-8 KNOT

DRIVE STAKE IN WITH MALLET

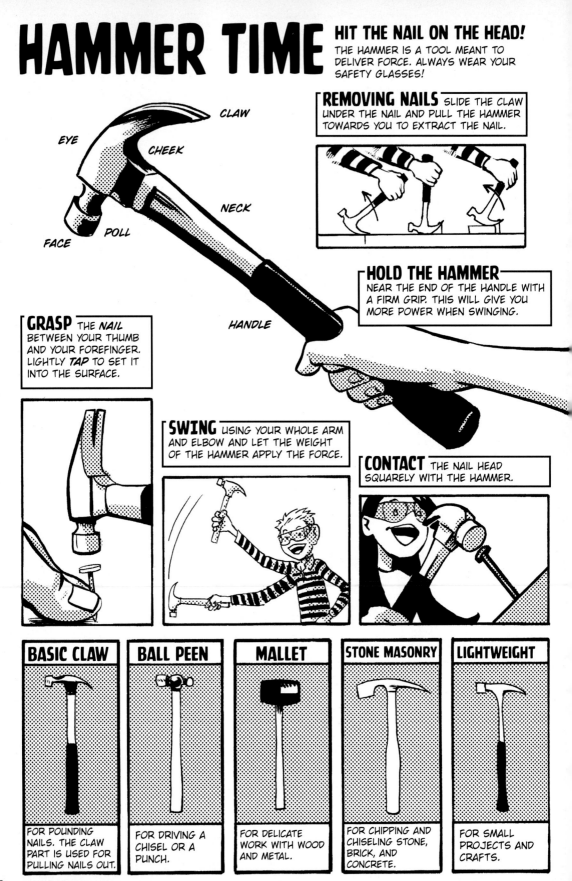

HAMMER TIME

HIT THE NAIL ON THE HEAD!
THE HAMMER IS A TOOL MEANT TO DELIVER FORCE. ALWAYS WEAR YOUR SAFETY GLASSES!

EYE

CLAW

CHEEK

NECK

FACE POLL

HANDLE

REMOVING NAILS
SLIDE THE CLAW UNDER THE NAIL AND PULL THE HAMMER TOWARDS YOU TO EXTRACT THE NAIL.

HOLD THE HAMMER
NEAR THE END OF THE HANDLE WITH A FIRM GRIP. THIS WILL GIVE YOU MORE POWER WHEN SWINGING.

GRASP
THE *NAIL* BETWEEN YOUR THUMB AND YOUR FOREFINGER. LIGHTLY *TAP* TO SET IT INTO THE SURFACE.

SWING
USING YOUR WHOLE ARM AND ELBOW AND LET THE WEIGHT OF THE HAMMER APPLY THE FORCE.

CONTACT
THE NAIL HEAD SQUARELY WITH THE HAMMER.

BASIC CLAW
FOR POUNDING NAILS. THE CLAW PART IS USED FOR PULLING NAILS OUT.

BALL PEEN
FOR DRIVING A CHISEL OR A PUNCH.

MALLET
FOR DELICATE WORK WITH WOOD AND METAL.

STONE MASONRY
FOR CHIPPING AND CHISELING STONE, BRICK, AND CONCRETE.

LIGHTWEIGHT
FOR SMALL PROJECTS AND CRAFTS.

CUT TO THE POINT

DOVETAIL SAWS
CLEAN, STURDY CUTS, GREAT FOR FRAMES, CABINETS AND TOYS.

BACK SAWS
THICK BLADED WITH REINFORCED BACK FOR PRECISION CUTS.

BOW SAWS
STEEL FRAME AND BLADE FOR ROUGH-CUTS OF WOOD.

CUTTING

LINE OF ACTION

THIS IS THE CORRECT CUTTING POSITION. YOUR VISION SHOULD ALWAYS BE TRUE TO THE CUTTING PLANE AND ALWAYS KEEP A STRAIGHT LINE OF ACTION!

IF POSSIBLE USE A CLAMP OR A VISE TO HOLD YOUR PIECE AND STOP VIBRATION.

CROSSCUT SAWS
FOR CUTTING AGAINST THE GRAIN. CAN BE USED FOR MANY PURPOSES FROM LOGGING TO DETAILED CARPENTRY.

CROSS CUT TEETH
CROSSCUT TEETH ARE SMALL TEETH USED TO SEVER WOOD WHEN CUTTING ACROSS THE GRAIN.

RIP SAWS
FOR CUTTING WITH THE GRAIN. THE RIPPING ACTION OF THE SAW PRODUCES A COARSE RAGGED CUT WHICH MAKES THE SAW UNSATISFACTORY TO FINISH.

RIP TEETH
RIP TEETH ARE MEDIUM-SIZED TEETH DESIGNED TO SCOOP OUT WOOD FIBERS WHEN CUTTING WITH THE GRAIN.

1"
4 T.P.I.

T.P.I. STANDS FOR TEETH PER INCH! RULE OF THUMB: THE MORE T.P.I. THE HARDER THE MATERIAL THE SAW CAN CUT!

COMPASS SAWS
SMALL BLADE USED FOR CUTTING CURVED OR STRAIGHT HOLES.

KEYHOLE SAWS
INTRICATE CLOSE INSIDE WORK FOR SPECIALTY JOBS.

COPING SAWS
CUTS IRREGULAR SHAPES AND INTRICATE PATTERNS.

ALWAYS PROTECT YOUR EYES!

THE HACKSAW
CUTS PLASTIC / METAL / WOOD
MOST VERSATILE OF ALL SAWS

CUTTING ANGLES?
30°
USE A MITER BOX!

UPKEEP A LIGHT COATING OF OIL WILL MAKE BLADES LAST LONGER. BE CAREFUL NOT TO BEND YOUR SAWS. HANGING THEM UP IS A GOOD METHOD FOR STORAGE.

OIL

SEE SAW

A SEE SAW IS A *LEVER*. THE LONG BOARD THAT HINGES ON A *PIVOT POINT* OF THE LEVER CALLED A *FULCRUM*. ALLOWING YOU TO LIFT OBJECTS THAT ARE MUCH HEAVIER THAN YOU COULD LIFT YOURSELF.

T-JOINT

PIPE NIPPLE

END CAP

6" GALVANIZED PIPE

HALF BURIED TIRE FOR A CUSHION.

FLOOR FLANGE

HANDLE BARS MADE OUT OF 1" X 6" GALVANIZED PIPE AND FITTINGS.

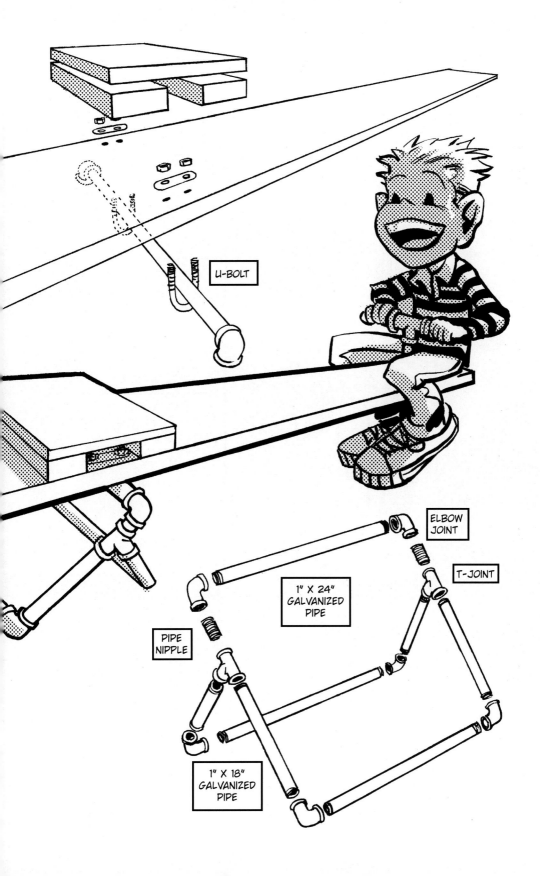

U-BOLT

ELBOW JOINT

T-JOINT

1" X 24" GALVANIZED PIPE

PIPE NIPPLE

1" X 18" GALVANIZED PIPE

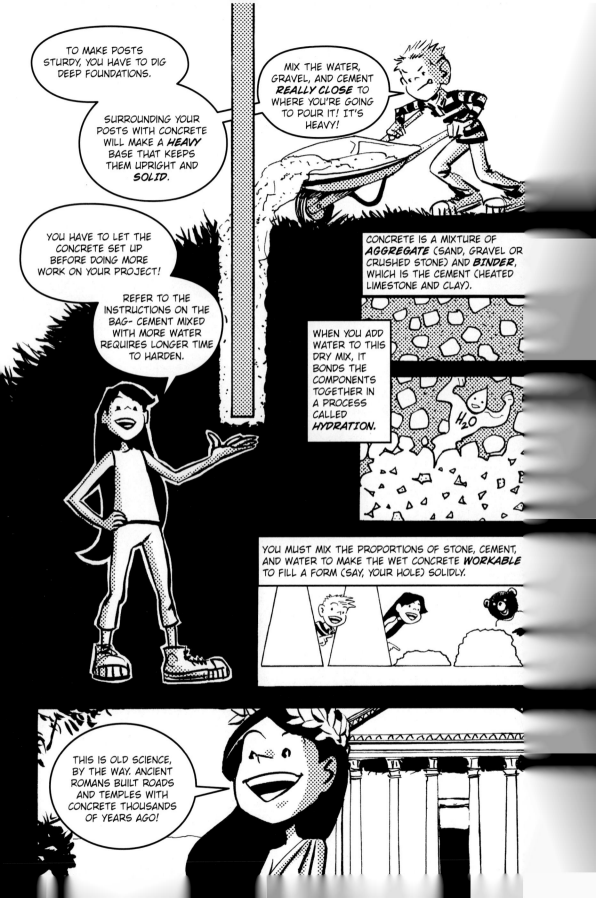

MONKEY BARS!

MATERIALS:
- (4) 4"X4"X10'
- (2) 2"X6"X10'
- (2) 2"X4"X8'
- (9) 20" 1" GALVANIZED METAL PIPE
- EPOXY ADHESIVE
- (24) 3 1/2" WOOD SCREWS
- (8) CARRIAGE BOLTS
- PREMIXED BAGGED CONCRETE
- MULCH

TOOLS:
- DRILLS AND BITS
- MALLET
- LEVEL

1 LADDER

NOTCH 4X4

6"

2"

USE A LEVEL TO MAKE SURE THE LADDER IS STRAIGHT.

DRILL 2 1/2" HOLES INTO THE BOARDS

SAW THE STEPS FOR THE LADDER

USING 3 1/2" WOOD SCREWS, USE THE SCREWDRIVER ATTACHMENT TO DRILL IN 2 SCREWS PER SIDE OF EACH STEP.

SPREAD MULCH UNDER THE MONKEY BARS FOR A SOFTER LANDING.

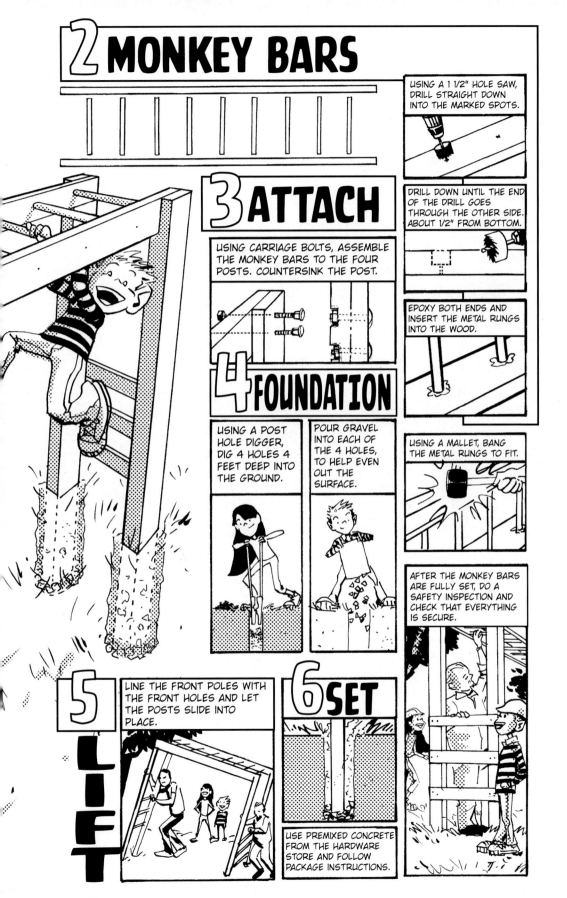

2 MONKEY BARS

3 ATTACH

USING A 1 1/2" HOLE SAW, DRILL STRAIGHT DOWN INTO THE MARKED SPOTS.

DRILL DOWN UNTIL THE END OF THE DRILL GOES THROUGH THE OTHER SIDE. ABOUT 1/2" FROM BOTTOM.

USING CARRIAGE BOLTS, ASSEMBLE THE MONKEY BARS TO THE FOUR POSTS. COUNTERSINK THE POST.

EPOXY BOTH ENDS AND INSERT THE METAL RUNGS INTO THE WOOD.

4 FOUNDATION

USING A POST HOLE DIGGER, DIG 4 HOLES 4 FEET DEEP INTO THE GROUND.

POUR GRAVEL INTO EACH OF THE 4 HOLES, TO HELP EVEN OUT THE SURFACE.

USING A MALLET, BANG THE METAL RUNGS TO FIT.

AFTER THE MONKEY BARS ARE FULLY SET, DO A SAFETY INSPECTION AND CHECK THAT EVERYTHING IS SECURE.

5 LIFT

LINE THE FRONT POLES WITH THE FRONT HOLES AND LET THE POSTS SLIDE INTO PLACE.

6 SET

USE PREMIXED CONCRETE FROM THE HARDWARE STORE AND FOLLOW PACKAGE INSTRUCTIONS.

ROPE LADDER

MATERIALS:
- 24 FEET OF 1/4" ROPE
- (8) 18"X1 1/2" HARDWOOD
- WOODEN RODS
- DUCT TAPE
- (2) EYELET SCREWS

NOW THAT OUR MONKEY BARS ARE BUILT LET'S ADD A LADDER!

MEASURE AND MARK 2" FROM EACH END OF THE WOODEN RODS.

2"

DRILL 1/4" HOLE IN EACH END OF THE RODS.

WRAP BOTH ENDS OF ROPE TIGHTLY WITH DUCT TAPE.

TIE A *DOUBLE OVERHAND STOPPER KNOT.*

① ② ③

TIE KNOTS SO THAT THE CENTER OF THE RODS ARE 12" APART.

12"

LET'S CONNECT THE LADDER USING A *SCAFFOLD KNOT.*

TIE A *SCAFFOLD KNOT*

① ② ③

④ ⑤ ⑥

SECURE BOTTOM OF THE LADDER USING STAKES.

PULL TO TIGHTEN THE KNOT

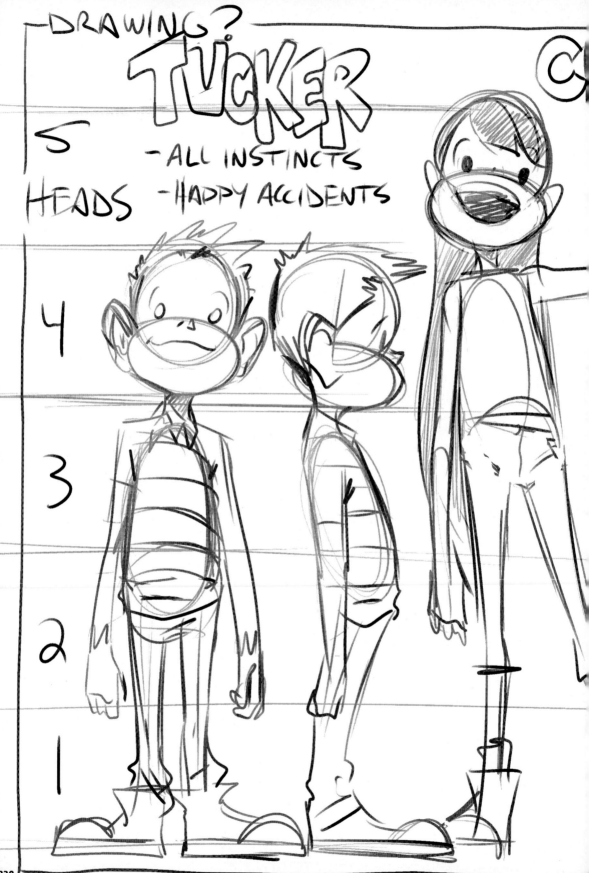

DRAWING?

TUCKER
- ALL INSTINCTS
- HAPPY ACCIDENTS

5

HEADS

4

3

2

1

INE –ANALYTICAL
       –THOUGHTFUL

HEADS

CIRCLE
OVAL
CARVE CHINS

PEAR
SHAPED
–BODY

SOLID
SHAPE
FOR HAIR!!

In the best engineering firms, design companies, and science research centers in the world there is always an interplay between art and technology. Great art inspires scientists and engineers to build the things that writers and artists dream up, while great science and engineering inspires artists with new potential plots and imagery. This interplay is age-old, and really the disciplines are two sides of the same creative coin, imagining new things, bringing them into existence, and sharing with the world. Aside from the creative collaboration around Howtoons, Nick and Ingrid help Saul in his professional life at Otherlab, a research laboratory, to visualize ideas early in the process, which enables more people to think about the early-stage concepts and contribute to and refine them. Visualization is a critical component of invention.

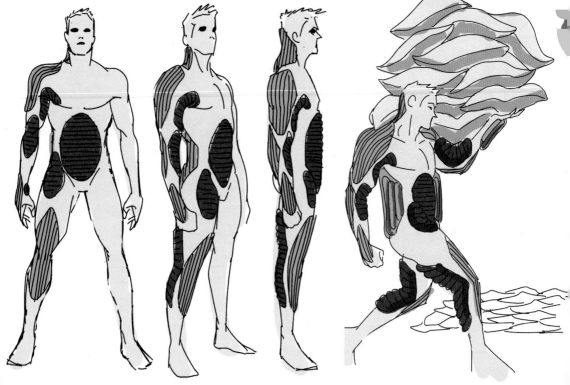

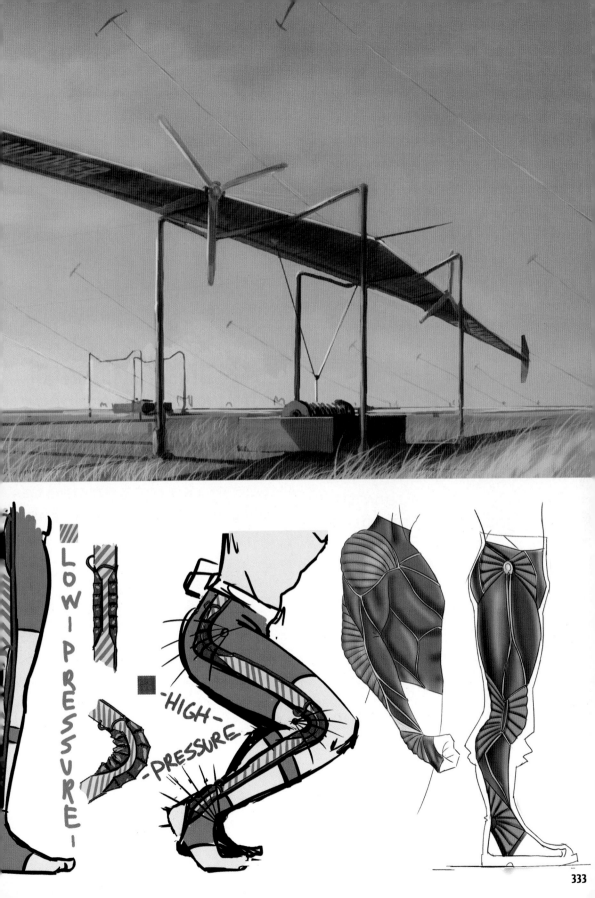

LOW PRESSURE

-HIGH-
-PRESSURE

GLOSSARY

ACTUATOR: An actuator converts energy into motion. Motors and hydraulic and pneumatic pistons are the things we most often think of as actuators but there are even more kinds… the muscles in our body are the actuators that help us move.

AERODYNAMICS: This is the study of the way that objects move through gases such as air. An object can be considered highly aerodynamic if it meets with little resistance, or "drag," as it moves through air.

ANCHOR: a rigid point of support, whether for securing a boat or a rope.

ARMATURE: The rotating coil in electric motors and generators. In our motor, it's the 10 loops of copper wound around the battery.

ARBORIST: Also known as a tree surgeon. They are lucky people who get to climb trees all day and care for them. Kind of like vets for plants.

BASSO: A deep, low singing voice.

BEND: A knot tying two lines (ropes) together.

BIGHT: When you bend a piece of rope to make a knot, it is called a bight. This U-shaped section of rope is useful in forming many knots. Threading the end of the rope around or through the bight is what creates the knot.

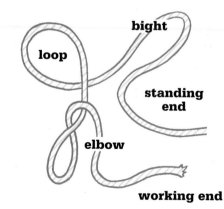

BINARY: describes a system that has two parts or modes (on or off, black or white, 1 or 0). Binary describes the base 2 counting system employed at the heart of modern computers.

BIT: This is the fundamental unit of computation as we know it. It is the name for the 1, or the 0, in binary digits.

BOOB TUBE: This is an antiquated, derogatory term that the artist's mother used to describe a television to those who watched it too much.

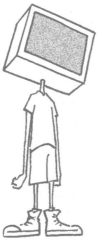

BRAID: Three or more things can be interwoven into a braid. Ropes and hair are often braided, but rarely together!

BRAINSTORMING: A method to produce lots of ideas, many bad, hopefully some good, in a short period of time.

BYTE: 8 bits in a row are called a byte. 00100001 is a byte that represents 132.

BUOYANCY: The ability or tendency to float in a fluid. We usually think of buoyancy in terms of boats and submarines in water, but buoyancy also applies to airships in air!

CENTIMETER: 1/100th of a meter. It is a commonly used unit in metric measurement. There are 2.54 centimeters in one inch.

COMMUTATOR: The device that switches the direction of current in the armature of an electric motor so that it is always going one way.

COMPRESSED AIR: Air that is pressurized more than the air around us.

CONDUCT: This term is used in science to describe movement through things. Heat conduction describes the movement of heat through a material. Electrical conduction is the movement of charge (or current) through a material.

COUNTERSINK: A counter-sink is related to the drill bit. It is used to widen the hole at the surface and to taper it such that the head of the crew or bolt can be hidden, recessed, or made "flush" with the surface.

CURRENT: In the same way that current describes the flow of water in a river, it describes the flow of charge in electric circuit.

DIMENSION: A dimension can be a measure of some-thing, like a length, width, or thickness. A dimension is also a property of space, like the three spatial di-mensions (up/down, left/right, forward/backward). Also of course, the 4th di-mension... Time!

DRAINAGE: The process of draining the liquid from something. Allowing the water to flow to the bot-tom of your terrarium is drainage for the soil on top.

ECOSYSTEM: In ecology, an ecosystem describes all the living and non-living things in an area. The bac-teria and dust in your na-vel (or belly button) might be described as its own ecosystem.

ELECTRICAL CIRCUIT: A col-lection of wires and com-ponents that electricity can pass round to perform some task. If the circuit is complete, electricity will be able to flow and make something happen.

ELECTRICAL CURRENT: The rate at which electrical charge flows through a cir-cuit, measured in amperes.

EMBOUCHURE: The shaping of the lips and movement of face mus-cles required to make wind instru-ments work.

ENTOMOLOGY: If you love ants, bees, and cockroach-es, entomology is for you. Entomology is the study of insects.

FOOT: 12 inches long, or 12 x 2.54 = 30.48 centimeters. Very Few people have feet that are a foot long.

FORCE: A mysterious power that gives Luke and Darth Vader their amazing skills. More seriously, force is an acceleration applied to a mass, which is a fancy way of describing pushing something.

FOSSIL RECORD: In the layers of earth beneath us lie the amoeba, plants, and dinosaurs that used to live on Earth. The order of the layers tells us much about our orgins. 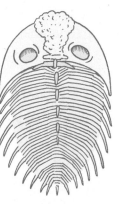 The fossil record resembles a layered cake of history, with the oldest layer on the bottom.

FOUNDATION: the lowest load-bearing part of a building, typically below ground level.

FREEZING POINT: This is the temperature at which a liquid, such as water, turns into a solid, such as ice.

FRICTION: Friction is more important than you think. Without friction, nothing would stick to anything, even temporarily. Everything would slide over everything like ice skates on a frozen lake. Things would never stand still. Friction you can then imagine, is really important. Friction is the way one surface resists another as they move over each other in contact.

FULCRUM: The point around which a lever rotates. The fulcrum is the place in the middle of the see-saw that squeaks when it's rusty.

FUSELAGE: The body section of an airplane.

FUSELAGE

GALVANIZED: A layer of zinc that coats iron or steel is "galvanized."

GAUGE: A tool for making measurements, like a pressure gauge, or a strain gauge, or a fuel or gas gauge.

GENERATOR: A generator converts one type of energy to another. The most common one we associate with the word is an internal combustion engine spinning a dynamo to make electricity.

GRAVITY: The force between two masses. The earth has a huge mass, which means it has a strong force that pulls your small mass toward it. This has an unfortunate tendency to make you fall toward the ground.

GYROSCOPE: A device with a spinning wheel at the center that can be used to determine changes in direction.

HESSIAN SACK: Also known as burlap, hessian is a heavy woven fabric made principally from jute and other vegetable fibers.

HITCH: A hitch is any form of knot that ties off to a post or ring.

HORIZON LINE: Assuming the picture plane stands vertical to ground, and **P** is the perpendicular projection of the eye point **O** on the picture plane, the horizon is defined as the horizontal line through P. The point P is the vanishing point of lines perpendicular to the picture.

HYDRATION: The addition of water in order to have the water be chemically absorbed.

HYDROPHOBIC: Hydro pertains to water, phobic means you don't like something. Hydro-phobic can then be understood as a distaste for water. A hydrophobic surface tends to repel water.

ILLUSION: A trick of the mind, eye, or ear that allows something to be perceived incorrectly.

INCH: 1/12th of a foot.

INSULATOR: Thermal insulation slows the flow of heat, while electrical insulation slows the flow of electricity.

LENS: Lenses are often transparent, and are used

to manipulate waves. That's a fancy way of saying they focus and divert light in interesting ways. Of course you can also focus and divert sound waves and ocean waves in similar ways with very different-looking lenses.

LEVER: a rigid bar resting on a pivot, used to help move a heavy or firmly fixed load with one end when pressure is applied to the other.

LIPID: A lipid is a molecule that doesn't like water. It includes fats and waxes. These useful little molecules do everything from storing energy to creating cell membranes.

MAGNET: Originally found in Magnesia in Ancient Greece, the word magnet came to describe materials where a magnetic polarity could be stored. The magnetic poles act upon each other to exert force, either attracting or repelling each other. NORTH   SOUTH

MASS: The mass of an object is kind of like the weight, except that it doesn't change if you move to planets with less gravity whereas your weight does.

METER: The international standard unit of length. There are 100 centimeters in a meter.

METHANE: Methane is one of the simplest fossil fuels: it's a gas (and the largest portion of natural gas). It's colorless and odorless. It is contained in your farts, but the smell comes from sulfurous compounds!

MILLIMETER: 1/1000th of a meter. There are 25.4 mm in an inch. 10 mm in 1 cm.

MOUNTAIN-FOLD: A mountain fold is the other fundamental fold of Origami. Again, like

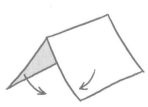

it sounds, a mountain fold is a fold that rises out of the paper, the way a mountain rises out of the landscape.

NUTS: Nuts screw onto screws, or bolts. They are often hexagonally shaped donuts with a screw thread in the middle. Like 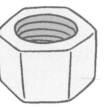 donuts, the right one can be hard to find when you need it.

OBSERVATION: Looking and studying something or someone very carefully to gain insight.

OCEANOGRAPHY: This is the study of the oceans and the seas of the world. It is becoming increasingly important in terms of understanding global warming and the heating of the oceans. More than 70% of the earth is covered in water; most of it is in the oceans.

PARABOLIC REFLECTOR: A mirror or reflecting surface shaped like a parabola.

Conveniently a parabola has a single focal point such that incoming light can be intensely focussed.

PERSISTENCE OF VISION: It's not just a recurring dream. Persistence of vision is the phenomenon by which some scientists believe we can create movement from a series of still pictures. It's still an open question for debate, so become a scientist and figure it out.

PERSPECTIVE: To draw and represent the three dimensional world, in two dimensions, accurately such that we perceive the images as realistic.

PHOTON: A photon is the simplest component of light. It is one of the fundamental particles. Photons move at the speed of light and are rarely seen alone…

PICCOLO: This is a fancy Italian word for a small flute, but can refer to any tiny musical instrument.

PLANE: Mathematically a plane is a two-dimensional surface, like a sheet of paper. A plain sheet of planar paper can be folded into a paper plane. A three-dimensional paper plane can fly.

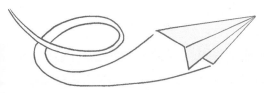

PNEUMATIC: A machine or system that runs on pressurized gas, typically air. Can be as simple as the pneumatic tire on your bike!

POLLUTE: A foreign or toxic item in an ecosystem is a pollutant. Pollution should be recycled or reused rather than tossed into the environment where they pollute.

PRESSURE: Pressure is a force that acts on an area or a surface. Your foot exerts pressure on the ground. The air in a tire exerts pressure against the walls of the tire.

PRIMARY COLOR: We know of red, yellow, and blue, as the 'primary' colors that when mixed can create (nearly) all of the other colors.

PROPORTION: The fraction of something that is part of the whole thing. For example the proportion of your body that is your head is about 1/6.

PVC: Polyvinylchloride is the plastic material more commonly known as PVC. It is used a lot in construction, and sometimes in the construction of toys.

RATCHET: A simple machine that uses a mechanism to allow free motion in only one direction. A zip tie is a simple example of a ratchet.

ROBOT: A robot is a machine that is programmed to do things. They eat, sleep, and dream in binary.

SAFETY PROTOCOL: A set of guidelines to help you do things safely.

SECONDARY COLOR: Secondary colors are mixtures of any two primary colors:

orange (yellow + red), purple/violet (red + blue), and green (blue + yellow).

SCOPE: This is the suffix for many technical instruments used to look at or observe something, such as microscopes and telescopes.

SHEARS: The general term for big scissor-type things. Because of their large handles with lots of leverage, they can cut things.

SIGN LANGUAGE: Combines hand shapes and positions into an entire language that is often used by deaf people.

SONIC: Not a hedgehog, rather things relating to sound waves.

STABILITY: If something is steady, unmoving, or stable, it is said to have stability.

SYMMETRICAL: An object is symmetrical, or has symmetry, when it is a reflection through a plane or a rotation around an axis. Your face is mostly symmetrical around the plane of your nose. A soda bottle is symmetrical about the axis that runs from the center of the base to the center of the cap.

THERMODYNAMICS: This is the branch of physics that studies the movement of energy, often in the form of heat, in a system.

TRANSLUCENT: Like transparent, except that the light rays passing through are scattered, and the objects on the other side are not clear.

TRANSPARENT: Something that light rays can pass through, and hence we can see clearly what is on the other side.

TUBULAR: In surfing, the most sought-after waves have a tube that can be ridden inside. The perfect waves are tubular, hence tubular is slang for awesome.

TURBINE: A turbine is a wheel that spins in a fluid, most often air or water. It can be used to extract energy, or to pump the fluid.

TYVEK: Is a brand name for polyethylene fibers in a sheet form. It's sort of like stretched milk bottles made into something like paper, except it is super strong and waterproof and very useful for all sorts of things.

VALLEY-FOLD: A valley fold is a fundamental fold of Origami. A valley fold is just like it sounds, a fold that goes into the page, the way a valley goes into the landscape.

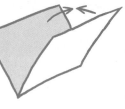

VANISHING POINT: The point at which all the lines viewed in perspective appear to converge, typically far out on the horizon.

VOLTAGE: The measure of the electrical potential of something. The more volts, the more jolts.

WEAVING: Two sets of threads are woven together to create fabric; the process is called weaving. The warp is the direction the weave comes out of the weaving loom, and the weft is the thread that passes along the

length of the loom. You can remember that the weft goes west (if the warp goes north to south!).

WOOD GRAIN: The patterns in a piece of wood caused by the alignment or growth direction of the wood fibers.

YARD: 3 feet or 36 inches long. A yard can also be a great place to play in, and should be many yards long.

INDEX

CELINE AND TUCK'S PARENTS PUT THEM TO SLEEP FOR CENTURIES TO RIDE OUT THE ENERGY CRISIS -- BUT WHEN THEY AWAKE IN THE FAR FUTURE AND MOM AND DAD ARE MISSING, IT'S THE KIDS WHO HAVE TO SAVE THE DAY!

GET ENERGY LITERATE IN...

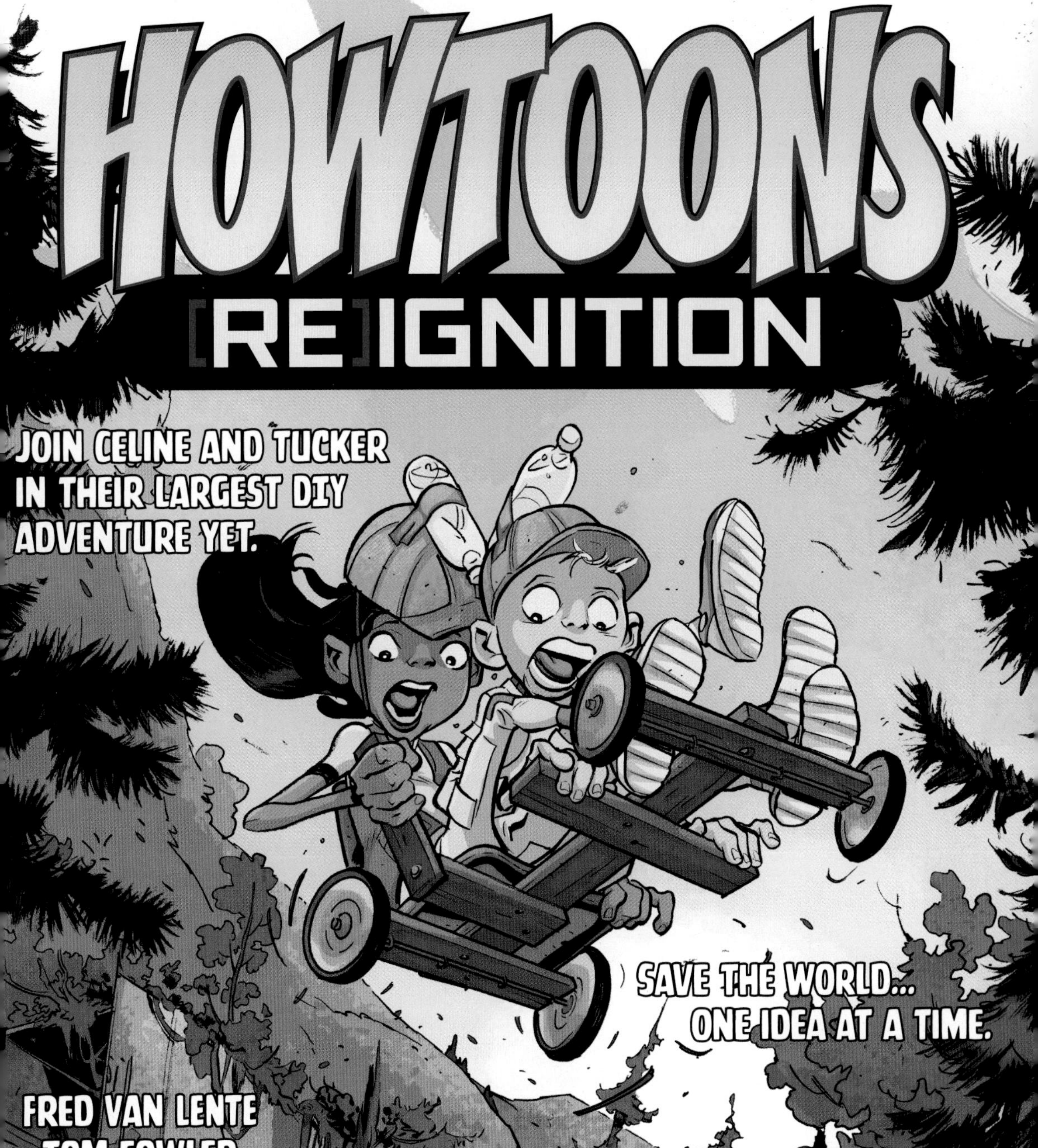

HOWTOONS
[RE]IGNITION

JOIN CELINE AND TUCKER IN THEIR LARGEST DIY ADVENTURE YET.

SAVE THE WORLD...
ONE IDEA AT A TIME.

FRED VAN LENTE
TOM FOWLER
JORDIE BELLAIRE

HOWTOONS [RE]IGNITION
VOL. 1 TP · 978-1-63215-056-1

imagecomics.com

This book is dedicated to Leo and Luc, Huxley and Bronte, and to all of the Howtooners who have helped and inspired us over the past 10 years!

SPECIAL THANKS...

Tim Anderson
Rhett Applestone
Autodesk
Elizabeth Bewley
Jim Capobianco
Aaron Carambula
Comicraft
Cooper Hewitt
Charlie Dunlap
Judith and Dom Dragotta
Leigh Estabrooks
Exploratorium
Pamela, Ross, and Selena Griffith
Ayano Hattori
Cameron Holland
Image Comics
Instructables
Cassie Jones
Amy Landis
Lemelson Foundation
Make Magazine
James McBride
Ryan McKinley

MIT-InvenTeams
MIT Media Lab
Munkhtur Family
Judith Regan
O'Reilly Foundation
Lorraine Palmer
Zola Volsan Rodgers
Gemma Rodriguez
Roland & Ahkylin
Daniel Rosenberg
Joel Rosenberg
Rumpus
Kristin Sabena
Patricia Sabena & Daniel Ahern
Joshua B Schuler
Science Museum Minnesota
Michelle Sharpswain &
Madison, WI Howtoons -
Summer Camp Crew
Star Simpson
Filiz Soyak
Eric Stephenson
Tiger

Dr. Saul Griffith is known as an inventor, but was trained as an engineer. He received his PhD at MIT. Since then Saul has used his training and skills to start numerous technology companies and has consistently championed STEAM education (including the A for ART!). Saul is currently running Otherlab, an independent research lab in San Francisco working on renewable energy, robotics, and advanced manufacturing technologies. Saul has been awarded numerous awards for invention including being named a MacArthur Fellow in 2007. Saul has dozens of patents in fields from aerospace to nanotechnology and enjoys being broadly trained as well as narrowly focused.

Nick Dragotta began his career at Marvel Comics working on titles as varied as X-Statix, The Age Of The Sentry, X-Men: First Class, Captain America: Forever Allies, Vengance, Fantastic Four #588, and FF. In addition, Nick is the co-creator and artist of the New York Times bestselling and Eisner nominated comic series East of West, with Jonathan Hickman at Image. He also works with Otherlab visualizing concepts.

Ingrid Dragotta is the designer and project manager for Howtoons. She also works as a designer for Otherlab. She earned her BFA in Product Design from the Savannah College of Art and Design and a DMBA in Design Strategy at California College of the Arts. Before Howtoons, Ingrid worked in the children's apparel and toy industries at New Balance Athletic Shoe Inc. and Hasbro, Inc.